TRIUMPH
TIGER 1C
AND DAYTONA

TRIUMPH
TIGER 100
AND DAYTONA

THE DEVELOPMENT HISTORY
OF THE PRE-UNIT AND UNIT
CONSTRUCTION 500cc TWINS

J R NELSON

First published by G. T. Foulis & Company in 1988, reprinted 1991.
Reprinted by Haynes Publishing in 1998.

British Library Cataloguing-in-Publication Data:
A catalogue record for this book
is available from the British Library

ISBN 1 85960 428 5

Library of Congress catalog card No. 88-82507

Haynes Publishing, Sparkford,
Nr Yeovil, Somerset, BA22 7JJ

Tel. 01963 440635 Fax: 01963 440001
Int. tel: +44 1963 440635 Fax: +44 1963 440001

E-mail: sales@haynes-manuals.co.uk
Web site: http://www.haynes.com

Haynes North America, Inc.
861 Lawrence Drive, Newbury Park,
California 91320 USA

Printed in Great Britain

Preface

It is almost ten years since 'Bonnie' was compiled (the development history of the Triumph Bonneville), being a year by year detailed account of the visual and specification changes to the T120 model in drawings and photographs, primarily intended for the restorer and enquirer to establish the correct specification for each year of manufacture.

It is gratifying to have learned that the book has now become a reference volume for the trade and enthusiast alike, so little persuasion was required to begin work on a companion volume for the T100 model.

It will be appreciated that the unfolding Technical Development history is constructed from a master chart compiled from a year by year rolling specification of part numbers. Such a chart indicates where changes took place, and which other parts were associated with that change. The book itself explains those changes, and where applicable, details of interchangeability.

Due to the long period of manufacture which this book covers, repetition has been avoided by referring continuing and like specifications back to the description of the year of introduction. Also to maintain a reasonably handy size to this volume, it was decided to omit the Master Specification Chart as an appendix to this publication – and make it readily available as a separate booklet. It is, after all, much easier to have that information readily laid out and immediately visible before you when reading the book, than continually having to refer to an appendix at the back of the book and losing one's original place!

I do hope this work proves to be both interesting and useful to those who almost remember the early days, and instructive to those who are coming after, wanting to rebuild and tame their own Tiger.

John R Nelson

Acknowledgements

When setting out to compile the technical development history of a universally loved motorcycle such as the Triumph Tiger 100, it does not take long to realise that no matter how comprehensive one's own records may be for the period, gaps in continuity and questions of fact begin to accumulate as the work progresses. I am lucky that so many of my earlier colleagues shared in my experience of life with the Triumph Engineering Company at Meriden, and have been willing to offer their contributions and assistance in the compilation of this book.

I want to thank both my old friends and colleagues, Jack Wickes for his graphic descriptions, memorabilia and photographs of the early Edward Turner days at Triumph, recalled in the "Why T100" chapter, and Doug Hele for the unrestricted use of his treasure chest of racing stories and records providing that touch of reality and excitement to the "Daytona" chapter.

Once again, I must acknowledge with gratitude the many quests made by Ivor Davies into his own formidable library of photographs for the pictures I was otherwise unable to find. To Harry Woolridge and Hughie Hancox my grateful thanks in providing essential technical information bridging the inevitable 'missing links' in my own records.

I must also admit to the use of essential photographs from the Norton collection, from earlier Triumph Publications and from literature that may still retain some obscure historic copyright, or require specific acknowledgement.

If this offends, I apologise, but do feel that whichever the case, they all really form an integral part of the 'universal' Triumph heritage – the story of the T100, the subject of this book.

PART ONE

Why Tiger 100?

The Triumph name had become well established world-wide even before the commencement of the First World War in 1914, the company having been founded in 1885, primarily for the manufacture of cycles in London. Shortly thereafter (in 1888) it moved to the Midlands, in Coventry, to produce both cycles and motorcycles. Between 1914 and 1939 the company became an important and firmly-established pillar of the Coventry industrial and commercial scene, finally venturing into the manufacture of major international event-winning Triumph motor cars.

This story really commences at the period when the Triumph Company Limited hit financial collapse and faced closure during the great industrial slump in the mid-1930s. The bankruptcy was often claimed to have occurred as a direct result of the company's concentration to the exclusion of all else on the preparation of, and the costs dissipated during, three years of successful participation in the full calendar of four wheeled national and international car racing and competitive events.

Whatever the cause, the result was that John Y. Sangster, already the owner of Ariel Motorcycles, stepped in and rescued the motorcycle interest from the general collapse. Amongst those rescued at the same time (many of whom had foreseen the inevitable and had, in fact, already prepared their escape routes) was my old friend and colleague Jack F Wickes (Wicko!), whose personal notes, memories and photographs have been freely drawn upon throughout this book.

Jack had joined Triumph in 1931, not leaving until the closure in 1974, but reminds us that his father had for many years been in charge of the Motorcycle Packing and Despatch Department long before Jack had even set foot in, and joined, the Company. Even in those days the Triumph range of motorcycles were being exported to a well-established world-wide network of distributors and dealers. (It may well be appropriate here to remind the reader that Triumph invariably exported far more motorcycles than ever it sold in the home market, and an oft-forgotten fact is that in the mid and late 1960s over 80% of the

Johnson Motors – Colorado Boulevard – Pasadena, California – first to be the pre-war US distributors of Ariel motorcycles, and soon after to also distribute Triumph to the whole of the United States

production was being exported consistently, earning for the Company on two successive years the coveted Queen's Award to Industry for Exports). When Edward Turner was brought into the company from Ariel by Sangster, he joined as Chief Design Engineer, Jack Wickes was a young designer draughtsman who was persuaded to become a part of the new re-vitalised design team, and ultimately to become Turner's right-hand man, personal assistant, mind reader, familiar, and the sharpening stone that maintained the master's fine cutting edge.

8   Edward Turner – taken in 1927 at his office desk in the design department of Ariel Motors

Jack Wickes. Joined the Triumph Company in 1931, and led the design team throughout the Turner years, until the closure of Meriden in 1974

The previous range of motorcycle products had already been rationalised by A.A. Sykes in the early 1930s, and by 1934, with the arrival of that largely unsung motorcycle designing hero, Val Page, a complete new range of economical 250, 350 and 500cc, both side and overhead valve, single cylinder models had been evolved, culminating in a 'top-of-the-range' 650cc ohv side-by-side twin. But the finished products were still not piercing the gloom of the depression, and the Motorcycle Division continued to grind gradually to a standstill, with rumours of cessation of motorcycle production abounding.

By 1937, the Turner flair had produced from that range of lightweight single cylinder side and overhead valve-engined motorcycles a range of ohv models which were not only good looking, but also gave a brisk performance coupled with continuing reliability, a point so often emphasised by the motorcycle press riders of the day. From the 250cc 2H model, the 350cc 3H, and 500cc 5H models of this first period there is no doubt that the tough regime imposed by Turner, quoted by the current technical press as being Scrooge-like and penny pinching, had been applied with but one single objective in mind. That, quite simply, was to tempt new customers to purchase from his new, re-styled range of lively and reliable motorcycles, which were available at a price they could afford, thereby putting the Triumph Engineering Company firmly back onto its feet. So the small design team, headed by Turner, and now including Jack Wickes, introduced sports versions of the 250, 350 and 500cc models. A name rather than numbers was essential to identify this new overhead valve range with which Turner now personally identified himself. A name, he said, that should portray a "real swashbuckling" appeal – and with only minimal inspirational delay, the 'Tigers' appeared!

Hadn't Coventry been the centre of the wool trade in mediaeval times? and had not Coventry developed its own distinctive blue dye – from whence came the famous Warwickshire Bluecoats School? – and even perhaps Coventry City's own Sky Blues! The earlier established drab paint colours, the reds, greens, greys and blacks were gradually   9 retired, but Edward Turner was not to be satisfied with just having "turned the corner". There was still too much to be done – and not enough time in which to do it! That Val Page twin was too tall, for instance, and needed flexing-up. The new range of singles, although proving eminently successful in the market place, needed real life injecting into them.

So the new 250cc Tiger 70, 350cc Tiger 80 and the 500cc Tiger 90 were released, resplendent with new shaped chrome-plated petrol tanks with metallic silver-painted panels, double lined in blue and sporting chromed wheel rims also lined in blue and new handlebars with integral controls, all eye-catching improvements!

The following year, in 1938, the faithful Val Page 650cc twin appeared fully metamorphosed as the Edward Turner, 500cc ohv 'Speed Twin', itself a sensation for its day. Again it was a masterly exercise in constructing what Turner knew he wanted from what he'd got, with costings always in mind, and always from the lighter choice. The Page twin was compacted, lightened, and arranged to fit into the already existing 'B' range frame and gearbox assembly, thereby commonising front forks, both front and rear wheels, gearboxes, chaincases and other stock items. In fact, a quick dip into the 1939 replacement parts catalogue indicates that almost everything else but the major engine components were common throughout the entire production range.

The odd man out, however, was the Tiger 70, born originally of the earlier favourite, the L2/1. Turner's mathematics calculated that an equivalent of £5 was being given away "in each toolbox" with every machine sold at the prevailing retail price of the day – £38 . . . so ultimately this model had to go.

Almost before the ink was dry on the 1938 catalogue announcing the arrival of the 'Speed Twin' the men of Brooklands were already aiming their sights on the 500cc lap record. It was on 8th October this was claimed by I.B. Wicksteed riding a Speed Twin to which he had fitted a supercharger, and succeeded in lapping the outer circuit in 1 minute 24.8 seconds, averaging 118.02 mph in a heavy downpour of rain.

A worthy curtain-raiser to the 1939 catalogued range of machines, which now included the latest pride of the range, the sporting version of the 500cc ohv vertical twin cylinder Speed Twin, on which was bestowed the title of Tiger 100.

The first official road test on 16th November 1938 said simply *'it seems to combine all those qualities which motorcyclists have hoped for but seldom actually experienced'*. To be able to write that of any motorcycle in its first year of manufacture, whether today or even nearly fifty years ago, is worthy praise indeed – and this is the machine that is to be the subject of our unfolding story.

There seemed to be so many differing variants of the basic Triumph logo that 'E.T.' also had this drawn and dimensioned full size, so no one should transgress further.

TRIUMPH

The World's Pre-eminent Motor Cycle

The cover of the 1940 sales catalogue, with the slogan "The World's Pre-eminent Motor Cycle", a statement that Edward Turner was soon to update – now the bikes had been attended to!

Described as a flexible multi, capable of nearly 100 mph, with a combination of docility and all-out performance, it demonstrated in no uncertain manner that *'speed can be obtained from a well-designed twin without sacrificing that flexibility which is so necessary on a road-going motorcycle'* (Motor Cycling 16th Nov 1938).

An original factory catalogue photograph, cleaned up for publicity purposes, and converted from 1939 to 1940 condition by the artist. Note the 'cocktail shaker' silencers.

11

Both the Speed Twin and its sister ship, the Tiger 100, were proving to be a sensation in the market. The Press, public, police and military authorities were quoting freely of a 'new era' in motorcycling. Reports from the home, empire, colonies and foreign markets were pouring into the factory Publicity Department, containing details of winning reliability trials, hill climbs, competitions and races, with fastest laps, team awards and record-breaking speeds, so that there was now absolutely no doubt whatsoever that the fortunes of the company had been completely turned around.

One November night in 1940, along came a chap called Hitler and dropped a bomb right in the middle of it all, blowing the lot to smithereens! Factory, bikes, machinery, tools, jigs, fixtures, and even the drawings themselves. Nevertheless motorcycles were still required for the war effort – some-one had to hit back, hadn't they? It is a wonderful tribute to the British wartime spirit and ingenuity the way the charred, wet and tattered fragments of information were pieced together from the debris. Drawings were borrowed back from the suppliers, from quotations, from inside coat pockets and even drawer linings, until the Drawing Office had re-pieced together a three-dimensional jig-saw of enormous proportions.

The complete destruction of the Dale Street factory reduced all manufacturing potential to zero in one direct hit on the night of 14th November 1940

Meantime, wheelbarrow loads of sifted tubes, lugs, machines, tools and other manufacturing paraphernalia had been carted off to near-by Warwick, where the first brave efforts were being set-up to re-commence manufacture in temporary accommodation which became aptly named the 'Tin Tabernacle'. Spares were already being reproduced in early 1941, and by mid-June that year motorcycles were being assembled, tested, wrapped and consigned to His Majesty's armed forces.

In the background, in great haste, and deep in the forbidden "Green Belt" around Coventry a factory was being built at great speed, a 'shadow factory' for the manufacture of Triumph motorcycles. It was located in a village just off the A45 from Birmingham to

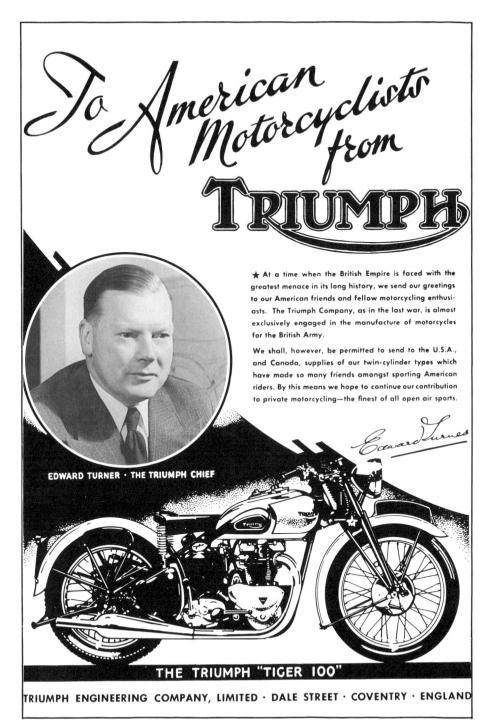

To American Motorcyclists from TRIUMPH

★ At a time when the British Empire is faced with the greatest menace in its long history, we send our greetings to our American friends and fellow motorcycling enthusiasts. The Triumph Company, as in the last war, is almost exclusively engaged in the manufacture of motorcycles for the British Army.

We shall, however, be permitted to send to the U.S.A., and Canada, supplies of our twin-cylinder types which have made so many friends amongst sporting American riders. By this means we hope to continue our contribution to private motorcycling—the finest of all open air sports.

Edward Turner

EDWARD TURNER · THE TRIUMPH CHIEF

THE TRIUMPH "TIGER 100"

TRIUMPH ENGINEERING COMPANY, LIMITED · DALE STREET · COVENTRY · ENGLAND

Edward Turner's hopeful message from Dale Street to North America in the early days of the war, when we had an Empire, Commonwealth, Protectorates and Colonies, and had just set out, almost alone, to fight for freedom

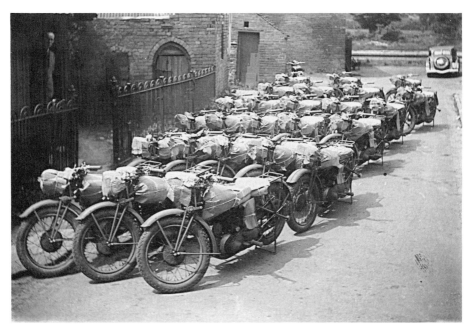

Production re-commences from the temporary premises at Warwick – machines packed and wrapped awaiting delivery for military use

Coventry, close to a place called Meriden (easier to pronounce than Allesley – the Postal District). Within ten months complete 350cc single cylinder motorcycles were being built there, and despatched away to 'do-their-bit'.

The twin engine continued under development, and was used for a number of wartime projects. One we understand was a one-man-tank device, discontinued having proved more dangerous to the user than the foe. Others included its use in portable ground generators and auxiliary hydraulic units, some of which exist today. The most successful appears to have been the 6kW auxiliary generating plant, often used airborne, legend having it responsible for more than one Lancaster bomber turning tail to have the fire extinguished!

The war ended, Triumph survived, and what was more, possessed a brand new modern factory in idyllic surroundings. However, the machinery wasn't new; it had been rebuilt and reconditioned piece by piece, bit by bit, by bearing and by bush. In many production areas the original overhead belt drive shafting and pulleys from the Dale Street holocaust had been reconditioned and re-installed in the new factory. What is perhaps more surprising and significant is that well over 40% of those very same machines were eventually sold at auction – still in fully-maintained working order at the final closure and demolition of the Meriden factory towards the end of 1983.

1946 dawned a new era – petrol was cheap, but in short supply and 'on coupons' until the end of May 1950! Motorcycles were an economical form of transport, cars almost unobtainable, and the end of the war meant freedom.

There was a tremendous shortage of manufacturing materials, but Triumph very rapidly resumed production of civilian motorcycles again, immediately re-establishing its pre-war distributors, agents and dealers throughout the world. 1946 also saw that incredible win by Ernie Lyons on the Freddie Clarke-prepared Tiger 100 based Grand-Prix model in the Senior Manx Grand Prix at an average speed of 76.74 mph over six laps. It ran on war-time 80 octane Pool petrol, with an 8.3:1 compression ratio, made possible by

14

6 kilowatt portable generator set with Metalastic rubber-type mounting feet

fitting an aluminium alloy cylinder barrel and head from a ground generator set on an otherwise mostly standard Tiger 100 engine bottom end.

Something like 200 of these models were built, with David Whitworth notching success after success on the Continent, culminating in D.G. Crossley repeating Ernie Lyons' Manx Grand Prix win just two years later, in 1948. Each machine was supplied with its own dynamometer bench test certificate, and each performed sufficiently well, world-wide, to clearly re-establish the almost forgotten pre-war Tiger 100 model on its rightful post-war pedestal.

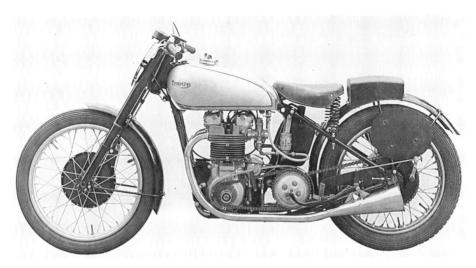

The 1946 GP Racer, photograph of the actual machine on which Ernie Lyons won the Isle of Man 1946 Manx 'Grand-Prix'

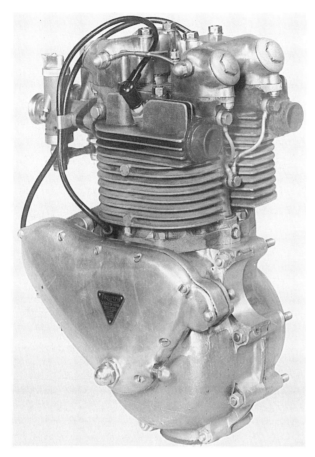

Production-type Tiger 100 'Grand-Prix' engine unit, utilising the bottom half of the standard Tiger 100 engine with aluminium alloy generator-type cylinder barrel and cylinder head, and fitted with twin Type 6 Amal carburettors, racing magneto, and ready for action!

(Below): An autographed action shot of David Whitworth, so successful on the Continental circuitry on his Grand-Prix model

Variation on a theme. Note that whilst the high speed boys were buzzing around the world's circuits with great success, the TR5 'Trophy' version was picking its way through trials and scrambles courses wherever they went!

Not wishing to catalogue the year-by-year changes to the Tiger 100, described in great detail elsewhere in this book, the post-war period did present grave difficulties for all manufacturers. Shortages of aluminium and copper, with chrome and nickel in particular, affected the quality of steels and protective and decorative finishes. Edward Turner stuck to his guns and would not have his Tiger 100 affected – all had to be fully up to specification. So you just had to wait if you wanted one! Customers did, and the waiting lists grew even though the policy of making a Triumph worth waiting for seemed to go on for years and years.

The Triumph Corporation East Coast Distribution Centre, set up by Denis McCormack in 1950 at Timonium, near Towson, Baltimore, Maryland, USA

Another Manx Grand Prix winner, Bernard Hargreaves, being congratulated by Edward Turner on his 1952 Clubman's TT win, whilst honeymooning. He actually crossed the finishing line with the rear wheel LH spindle nut missing altogether – and which was suitably plinth-mounted and presented by 'E.T.' at the celebratory dinner in honour of his victory

(Below): **TR5** goes swinging arm in 1953 – 500cc works scrambler

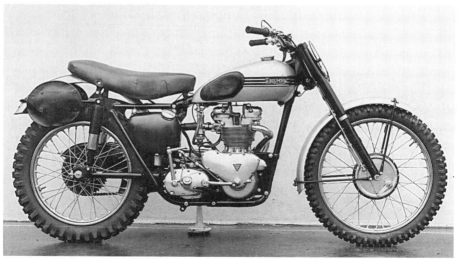

18

USA Class 'C' racer – no front brake – no spring hub – twin GP carbs, and 'let's-go!'

1946 saw the introduction of the Triumph telescopic front fork, 1947 the rear spring wheel, and 1949 the 'Nacelle'. In 1950 there was the new gearbox with its live layshaft and speedo drive, the aluminium close pitch finned cylinder barrel and head and the new twinseat following in 1951. A swinging arm frame became available in 1954. By 1959, the 'big brother' Bonneville had begun to steal the limelight and to hit the headlines, but other plots had already been thickening.

So it was not surprising that 1960 saw the emergence of a completely new type of 'over-square' lightweight unit-construction Tiger 100, given the unromantic nomenclature of T100A. This model too was to win its many battles and have bestowed its accolades before proudly claiming its ultimate title of Tiger 100 'Daytona'.

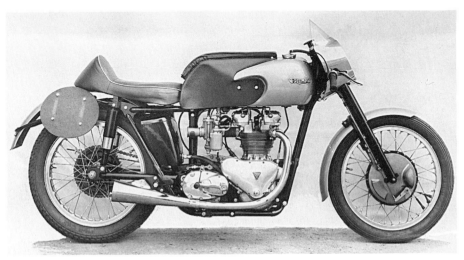

This photograph bears the legend – 1955, 500 for P.H. Tait. If so, a considerable amount of Frank Baker ingenuity and Stan Truslove care and skill would have been lavished upon it, Percy gaining success on success as the years rolled by

19

The first time the World Motorcycle Speed Record holder decal was applied to the nacelle was in 1956 following Johnny Allen's first confirmed World highest speed record ever achieved on a motorcycle on the 25th September 1955. The maximum speed achieved for the flying kilo was 193.72mph. On September 6th 1956 he increased this record to a speed of 214mph

PART TWO

Why Daytona?

Perhaps not everyone has heard of Daytona Beach on the eastern coast of the Florida Peninsula in the United States of America. For those who may have not, a brief whisper from the past history of motorcycle racing in America may not come amiss. Daytona Beach itself is just north of the Tropic of Cancer, faces the Atlantic Ocean, and has for aeons of time been drenched with the tropical sun and tides leaving mile after mile of pure white sand beaches, with a paved road running from north to south just above the high water mark.

Famous since 1937 for motorcycle sand racing, 'Daytona Beach' had already achieved National status by the time our story begins, when we simply record the winner of the 1950 event on his own 1949 Triumph Tiger 100-based Grand Prix as one Roger Mahon Coates. Later, he became known to everyone who subsequently ever handled a Triumph motorcycle east of the Mississippi as 'Rod' Coates, the Service Manager of the Triumph Corporation in Towson, Baltimore. Incidentally, the same machine, still bearing his original number 43, was prepared 34 years later by Coates in 1984, and ridden into first place by Russel Paulk in a relatively new type of event for the USA, a Vintage Classic Race, held at the new Daytona Beach International Speedway in Florida – during the speed-week events.

The present 3.81 mile raceway with its banked outer circuit provides superlative all-round spectator viewing, and is equipped with the latest in electronic information display and score boards, giving results and positions lap by lap and second by second – a magnificent circuit even on which to complete. A dazzling achievement to finish the race – but to win?

So why in February 1966 were four Triumph 500cc ohv twin cylinder Tiger 100 motorcycles sent from the factory in Meriden UK, to stand on the starting grid, where already the 750cc 'flat head' Harley-Davidson reigned supreme? Why choose Daytona, particularly in view of the fact that Triumph never raced, and didn't even support privateers racing their own Triumphs – except on very rare dubious and unofficial occasions? Even then if they had been successful, the employee responsible was usually officially 'disgraced' and subsequently consigned to Saudi Arabia (literally), or was forced to suffer similar sideways-type promotional displeasure – so why Daytona Beach, Florida, in March 1966? Edward Turner had by now relinquished command, and Harry Sturgeon, recently from DeHavilland Aircraft, had taken control. Edward Turner's report following his extended visit to Japan had already been presented to the Board and Sturgeon continued to study very closely the continuing Oriental progress, and in particular that of Honda.

TUE 751 consuming the miles necessary to prove a prototype ensured the durability the customer is not necessarily likely to be calling upon, as well as its eventual reliability.

Photograph taken in 1956 when David Jones had won the 25 mile novice race in Laconia, being congratulated by a very happy Rod Coates, Service Manager of the East Coast Distributors, the Triumph Corporation on Towson, Baltimore. (Historical note:- David Jones, a brother-in-law of Jack Wickes was already part of the Meriden experimental team, and was selected to transfer to the newly formed Triumph Corporation in Towson, Baltimore to provide the factory technical service back-up in 1950. He now resides in Florida).

This picture featured in the 1963 U.S.A. sales catalogue and was captioned "and if it's silverware you want, what better way of collecting it than on a Triumph!" The winner's name on the Jack Pine cow bell enduro trophy is Ken Penton.

Following a Board meeting in early 1965, which inevitably discussed the impending technological invasion of the USA and Europe, Bill Rawson, then Sales Director of BSA, forwarded to Bert Hopwood, the Deputy Managing Director and Technical Director of the BSA Group, the earliest available details of the forthcoming Japanese 450cc double overhead camshaft twin cylinder model – the CB450 Honda.

The covert supporting documentation in Japanese characters had been hastily transcribed into English to detail a top speed in full road trim of 180 kph (112 mph), a displacement of 444cc and a compression ratio of 8.5:1, providing 44 bhp at 8500 rpm. Supporting performance graphs gave a standing start figure of more than 100 yards in less than 5.3 seconds, and at that fully equipped with electric starter. A new yardstick with which to be beaten? What would this beastie do in full race trim?

Hopwood forwarded this information to Brian Jones, Doug Hele and Henry Vale on 22nd June 1965 – and not for passing interest either!

The rest of this story is told directly from Doug Hele's own private portfolio.

At a date remaining unrecorded, Doug was summoned into the Sturgeon/Hopwood presence to learn it had been decided that in order to retain the established sales ascendency, a major road race success had to be achieved by the Group. At the same time it had to be borne in mind the much discussed Hopwood 'Modular' series of engines based on 250cc fundamental increments destined to replace the current range of production models, including the Tiger 100, had not even yet left the drawing board. Furthermore, that there was no time to develop and manufacture for homologation (ie a sufficient quantity having been actually manufactured to a published catalogue specification) an overhead camshaft version (either single or twin cam) of the existing Tiger 100. The only competitive 500cc 23

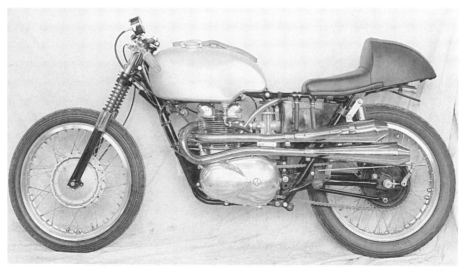

General LH side view of the 1966 Daytona T100 illustrating the extensive use of standard production components.

twin within the BSA group was the existing Tiger 100 – and that was to be the sole object of Doug's endeavours.

Oh! and furthermore Doug was told it should win the Daytona 200 Mile Experts Race in 1966 – Don Burnett had won it on a Tiger 100 in 1962, hadn't he, so he was given nine months to bring about a repeat performance, with the proviso that there was lots more expertise and eager hands in America to help him in his endeavours!

Well! It's not as easy as that! Being successful in production-type racing events, as the Tiger 100 certainly was, is a vastly different proposition from competing against the very best factory-entered racing machinery the rest of the up-and-coming new world can muster, already experience-fashioned following many hard racing miles of disasters and disappointments.

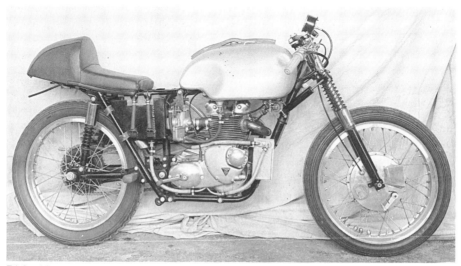

Right side view 1966 Daytona T100.

Anyway, here was something new! At the very least it was an instruction 'to get-on-with-it'. Fortunately it was no strange territory for Doug to have to explore, his previous Norton background of race-bred successes forming part of the tapestry of the Norton story itself.

Even so, fundamental changes had to be initiated into the existing design of the Tiger 100 if it were to be able to withstand the rigours of such an adventure, not least of which would be the basic race-way handling of the machine if and when equipped with a motor capable of delivering the necessary power. Such a frame had to be within the currently available manufacturing capabilities of Meriden at that time. The new frame therefore featured a new headlug incorporating an additional top bracing strut, with the rear swinging arm spindle now firmly located in position by two outboard stiffening and locating plates welded to the rear frame section. The swinging arm itself was reinforced and stiffened at the same time.

The power unit, although already proven durable, had not only now to provide much more horsepower but must be capable of delivering it at continuous maximum racing rpm, hour after hour. Work started straight away to provide better air/fuel mixture flow to the cylinder head, achieved by changing the valve angles from 40° to 38³/4°, thereby allowing larger diameter inlet (1.531 in) and exhaust (1.406 in) valves. 9.75:1 'pent-roof' pistons, dural valve guides, barrelled hollow alloy push rods, Tri-Cor (US) valve springs with standard top caps, lightened and polished rocker arms, (small adjuster nuts with redundant adjuster threads removed), in conjunction with modified BSA 'Spitfire' racing form camshafts and three inch radius cam followers formed the basic engine configuration.

The cylinder head now carried separate 1³/32 in bore 'bolt-on' adaptors to each 1³/32 in inlet port, connecting via 1¹/4 in. diameter canvas-reinforced rubber hoses to the 1.10 in diameter carburettor adaptors which flared for the last ³/4 inch to the 1³/16 inch diameter choke Amal GP carburettors with remote, rubber-suspended racing float bowls. The air bells were supported in foam from a bracket on the frame. The exhaust pipes were 1¹/2 in. o/d x 31 in into reverse cone megaphones with two inch outlets.

A substantial oil cooler was mounted forward of the engine on the right side, connected to the one gallon central oil tank, with formed cut-aways to accommodate the carburettor bellmouths.

A standard crankshaft assembly with a plain timing side oil feed journal and standard production specification connecting rods was used, in conjunction with a double lipped roller bearing on the drive side, within the standard crankcase assembly. However, some basic changes were introduced. The first was the deletion of the drive-side crankcase/ sprocket oil seal in favour of three ¹/16 in diameter drilled oil level holes to maintain a constant 250/300cc oil level in the primary chaincase. An Elektron timing cover located the exhaust camshaft-driven Lucas racing contact breaker unit, connected to the twin encapsulated Lucas 3ET energy transfer ignition coils mounted beneath the fuel tank forward mounts, fed directly from the encapsulated energy transfer stator within the primary chaincase. Additional lubrication was provided to the cam follower guide blocks to eliminate the previously experienced problems of camshaft wear.

Standard Triumph front forks and front and rear wheels with drum brakes, but with alloy wheel rims, were used, the front anchor plate sporting the obligatory air scoop and exit vent.

This is basically how the four Tiger 100s arrived in the USA in early March 1966, to await the arrival of Doug Hele just two weeks before the race to supervise the settling-in process. Their riders came from Jomo (Johnson Motors – the west coast Triumph distributors based at Pasadena – California, already with a formidable local reputation for racing successes) and from Tri-Cor (the Triumph Corporation east coast distribution centre, based at Towson, Baltimore). Each, of course were intent on out-doing the other. 25

for – as the song goes – 'East is east, and west is west' – and Doug just had to provide the goods so that no one lost!

Doug's record shows steady progress and consolidation towards a final specification between the 5th and 20th March, notwithstanding camshaft and follower failures, premature crankshaft main bearing problems, and the odd bits falling off during practice.

But Jess Thomas had already achieved 124 mph in very wet conditions, and Gary Nixon had completed 22 searing laps in one practice session.

Inevitably, the great day arrived on 20th March. Now at last, for the teams from Meriden, Baltimore and Pasadena, the 2 am., 3 am., and 4 am., strip, examine, modify and rebuild sessions were a thing of the past. Gone were the decisions whether to continue to use reliable standard or untried next generation technology, whether to listen to the others – where 'never the twain shall meet' or be guided solely by one's own logic.

Doug's own diary entry for 20th March 1966 reads: *Walk to the track – back to the garage for the spare fairing – watch the race with Mr Sturgeon (the Managing Director of the whole of the BSA Group who had only nine month's ago charged him with winning this event) – went to Motor Cycle Association celebration dinner and prize distribution. Note:- old-type Dunlop tyre most important for handling on our machines.*

But to the race itself. The Triumph team had high hopes, but inwardly no great expectations. It was the very first time 'for real'. The weather was beautiful as the 107 experts took to the field at the drop of the starter's flag. That great master Cal Rayborn on his factory-tuned 750cc Harley-Davidson side valve had already been fastest qualifier, and had gained 'pole' position, at 134.148 mph. From the word 'go' he forged ahead and even broke the track's first lap record! This was going to be a humdinger of a race! An unsung privately-entered Tiger 100, beautifully prepared by Woody Leone and ridden by Dick Hammer, sneaked past Rayborn on lap two, only to be overtaken again on lap three.

Elmore receives the trophy from the late Harry Sturgeon at the Daytona 66 prize giving celebration.

The Triumph Corporation had also prepared their own Rod Coates/Cliff Guild special, to be ridden by their very own Gary Nixon. By the thirteenth lap Gary took on the field with Roger Reiman now in second place.

Buddy Elmore, on his factory Triumph, had started way back on the line from 46th place, and being so far back in the field had completely escaped notice from that all-seeing official race commentator Roxy Rockwood. However, from lap 1 Elmore had been reducing the lead by two seconds a lap, so that by lap eighteen he had passed Reiman, and two laps later challenged Nixon to go into the lead, with George Roeder almost twenty seconds back in third place.

Triumphs were in positions one and two, with the usual reshufflings during pit refuelling stops, until the 44th lap when a puncture put Gary Nixon into the pits.

Even as Elmore received the chequered flag, the question still arose 'where the hell did he come from!' – but the lap scorers confirmed he was there all the time! To crown it all, despite his pit stop for puncture repairs, Gary Nixon came in ninth!

Doug Hele was seen to relax, Sturgeon to smile, but the latter was heard muttering about 'next year', and 'one-two-three'!

The strip report on Elmore's engine showed little real distress, with only slight wear to camshafts and followers, and no crankshaft problems, but Doug's notebook already contained enough observations to initiate next year's development programme.

This year's success was sufficient to ensure the US Triumph distributors publicity agents would re-name the 500cc winner the Daytona Tiger 100, a title the 1967 catalogue would be destined to carry. It was therefore inevitable that 1967 was to see a less hurried and better planned repeat attempt.

The prototype 1967 Daytona frame. Note the new head lug and triangulated top frame, and the bent frame tube under the gearbox to allow the proposed 'tucked-in' right side exhaust system. 27

The four 1966 bikes were left in the US to continue their successess gained at Daytona, but more importantly to continue to gain experience and information for the next generation machines now being developed in Coventry, where the dynamometers were being used to their fullest extent.

The standard 1967 season production model had already introduced the new frame with the immensely stiffer triangulated-type head lug, eliminating the previous swan-necked version with the 'add-on' bracing strut. By judicious shortening of this new frame top tube by about $3/4$ in, the effective head angle was thereby reduced to 63°, at the same time adding something like $1/2$ in to the trail, with an inherent bonus of bringing lower the centre of gravity. An immediate further handling improvement was achieved from the use of 18 inch wheels, which allowed a shortening of the front forks themselves. With the incorporation of the hydraulic shuttle damping valve it not only further lowered the centre of gravity, but provided rock steady stability at all speeds, and under all conditions. Finally, the fork yokes were altered to regain the original $3^3/8$ in trail, whilst the fork movement retained its standard $5^5/8$ in. The final road-holding improvement was provided by the enhanced stopping power of the Fontana twin drum, four leading shoe front brake, whilst retaining the standard Triumph seven inch single leading shoe rear – although the rear wheel was actually converted back to 3.50 x 19 in for the actual race event.

The oil cooler system was retained, but the fuel tank made narrower, and in glass reinforced plastic, to encourage the rider to nestle closer within the new style, lower and more aerodynamic-shaped fairing.

The 1966 Tigers had incorporated oil pressure feed to the camshaft and followers, but cam wear problems had been experienced, mainly due to a faltering oil supply caused as a direct result of crankshaft timing-side journal and bush wear, allowing oil pressure bleed, and hence loss of flow. For 1967 the timing side crankshaft and crankcase were altered to accept a ball journal bearing, with oil sealed oil pressure feed retention to the shaft and big-ends. Hard-faced camshafts and three inch cam followers were now used with

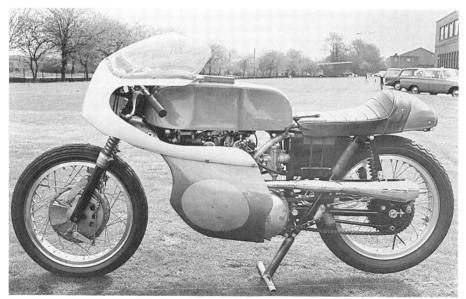

Left side view of the 1967 Daytona racing machine prior to despatch to the United States. Note the Fontana front brake, high level L/H exhaust system, restyled fuel tank seat and fairing.

'beefed-up' cylinder barrels against possible flange fracture in the light of increased torque provided by the higher compression ratio and squish type cylinder head format. Increased strength connecting rods were also introduced.

Work on the cylinder head provided additional support material around the valve guides, whilst inlet valve stem length allowed an improved valve spring fitted length. Induction tract lengths were altered to gain flexibility and improve performance, whilst the twin parallel Amal GP carburettors were mounted on a fixed plate as an integral unit with a centrally-mounted remote float chamber.

The gearbox now featured more advantageous ratios reasoned to be desirable for the Daytona circuit, and to gain the maximum advantage from the new power characteristic coupled with the added braking capability.

Three machines to the above specifications were handed to the team from Tri-Cor, comprising Gary Nixon, Larry Palmgren and Buddy Elmore, and three to the Jomo team consisting of Dick Hammer, Gene Romero and Eddie Mulder. All six machines had already been bench tested, road tested for at least twenty miles, and run at MIRA at speeds up to 130 mph. Mention must be made of the excellence of technical support provided by the Jomo West Coast Service Manager Al Stuckley, supported by Pat Owens and the World's Speed Record-breaker engineer Jack Wilson. They were backed up so ably by the 'local' East Coast Baltimore distributor squad led by their Service Manager Rod Coates and that maestro of engine building and tuning, Cliff Guild. Mention must not be omitted of the twenty-four hour support crew, chef, chief cook and bottle washer, nursemaid, time keeper and guardian angel, the one and only Marge Coates, who kept 'em all toeing the line!

The practising prior to the race went like clockwork, with almost military precision, and with none of the major set backs that had bedevilled the previous year. The six machines completed 360 practice laps between them, averaging 230 miles per machine. At the pre-race timed trials they finished in first, second, seventh, eighth, ninth and fifteenth placings, Dick Hammer taking pole position having clocked 135.746 mph, a mile and a half faster than the previous year's fastest qualifier, Cal Rayborn.

This year, 1967, the date was 19th March, and all was set for the start of the 200 mile experts race. As the starter's flag fell, both Hammer and Nixon drove out of the start lane side by side, first into the left hander, and on and on side by side, until the end of lap one, when they crossed the start-finishing line almost side by side, with an incredible three seconds lead on the following pack led by third man Buddy Elmore.

The pressure was really on, and was kept on lap after lap for the next hundred miles, Hammer keeping only just a wheel in front of Nixon. By this time the tail enders were starting to get in the way, causing the Hammer/Nixon pattern to change with almost each successive lap, until lap 26 when Hammer decided to pull into the pit lane to refuel. Nixon therefore moved into first place, Elmore taking over in third.

Dick Hammer made an excellent pit stop, but appeared to lose all steam on his return to the circuit. By the time the Triumph pit had overcome its panic, Hammer was back on full song again. It was later rumoured that Dick had borrowed some rag from a mechanic to clear his visor, and had trapped it on his seat as he re-started, only to have it restrict a carburettor until it finally dislodged and the orchestra returned to full song! By lap 27 Hammer had regained second place to Elmore's third. Nixon took his pit stop on the 30th lap and returned to retain his first place position, the pit crew having taken only seven seconds.

On the 29th lap Elmore made his re-fuelling stop, also without losing his place. Hammer was now pressing on to challenge for that No 1 spot, but overcooked it in the 31st lap when only four seconds behind the leader – Nixon. He took a 100 mph spill across the turf when making the critical turn leading to the infield. Within one and a half minutes he   29 was back on the track, weaving his way up through the back markers, and still managed to finish in seventh position! This signalled to Elmore the chance was still there to win, so over the remaining laps Elmore closed on Nixon, and by the end of the race, these two riders had lapped the entire field, and had each been unofficially turning in laps at over 100 mph. It was a strange sight to witness George Roder, the third man, actually being overtaken by our two heroes, Nixon and Elmore as he crossed the finishing line – with one full lap yet to go!

The winners' enclosure – a rapturous Gary Nixon (9) with Cliff Guide immediately on his right and Buddy Elmore (79) ably supported by his mechanic Dick Bender. Almost unseen amongst the supporting local beauty is Doug Hele pondering what might have been if only Dick Hammer hadn't taken the country route!

All six of Doug's machines finished in the first fifteen places out of the ninety seven starters. The Tiger 100 had now decisively re-affirmed its claim to the Daytona title, Doug's examination report on the winning machine read as if it were difficult to determine a positive problem – almost a list of observations on points that might benefit from some improvement. It concluded with the words: *we can still further improve our machines in many respects, and we must either do these or not return next year.*

It is here we should end our story – but life's not like that! Doug Hele's notes continue through 1967 to the drop of the flag at the 1968 Daytona event, with the same meticulous attention to detail, the same step by step incremental improvements. This year, for instance, the bikes were achieving over 144 mph during the timed trial. But somehow all was not well, which was sadly confirmed during the race. All of the Triumphs were bedevilled with misfires and fading performance, subsequently traced to internal failures within the new-type printed circuit encapsulated generator stators. Otherwise, who knows what the outcome might have been? This, my son, is the racing game!!

All was not lost. The features of the 1967 race-winning model rapidly found their way into the standard production model T100 Daytona by 1969. Even more significant was the fact that the newest model in the Meriden stable, 'the Tiger with the three cylinders' – the 750cc Trident – was to incorporate all those very features prepared for the 1968 event. When next engaged in combat on the battlefields of Daytona Beach in 1971, the Triumph entry was devastatingly successful. But that is yet again another story!

The happy winner of the 1967 Daytona 200 mile expert's race – Gary Nixon. Immediately after one of the many radio and TV interviews held in the melée of the winners' enclosure, Gary quietly turned to me and said "Ye know Mister Nelson, I managed to say the name Triumph thirteen tarms in that interview!"

PART THREE

1939-1959
Pre-Unit Construction
T100
Year-by-Year
model description

1939 Triumph T100 Tiger 100.

1939 model: Triumph T100 Tiger 100 Twin
Commencing Engine Number: 9-T100 followed by the series number
Model: T100
Associated 'B' range model: 500cc 5T model 'Speed Twin'

Engine

Based on the immensely successful 500cc Speed Twin model introduced in 1938, the Tiger 100 was marketed in 1939 as the 'super' high performance version of that same 63 mm bore x 80 mm stroke, 498cc overhead valve transverse vertical twin cylinder machine. Like the Speed Twin, it was equipped with "double high camshafts" and had a built-up crankshaft with centrally mounted flywheel which was supported on ball journal bearings within the vertically-split high tensile aluminium alloy crankcase assembly. Pressure oil lubrication was fed from a twin parallel plunger (feed and scavenge) Triumph oil pump within the timing chest, to the forged RR56 aluminium alloy connecting rods with machined big-ends, having Babbit white metal-lined steel end caps. A threaded boss at the forward edge of the timing case cover provided a feed to the rocker boxes via a screw-metered restrictor valve, which itself incorporated a by-pass tapping pipe to the tank instrument panel-mounted oil pressure gauge. Forged aluminim alloy split skirt 7.75 compression ratio pistons were used in conjunction with twin compression and single oil scraper rings. The twin bore cylinder barrel was in cast-iron, as was the twin hemispherical combustion chamber cylinder head. Separate oil pressure fed aluminium alloy inlet and exhaust rocker boxes bolted directly onto the cylinder head, locating and sealing into position the chrome-plated push rod cover tubes, into which drained the oil from the valve cavities via external pipe lines from the cylinder head. A one inch Amal type 76 carburettor was specified, fitted with a bell mouth. Ignition was provided by a Lucas Magdyno with handlebar-controlled advance and retard mechanism.

Gearbox

The four-speed gearbox, produced under Triumph's own patents, featured fully enclosed positive stop right side footchange mechanism, and comprised gears and shafts of nickel-chrome steel, the fully floating layshaft supported at each end in phosphor bronze bushes.

Primary Transmission

The single row $^3/_8$ in pitch primary chain ran in a sealed and polished cast aluminium alloy oil bath   33

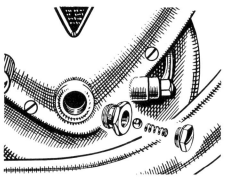 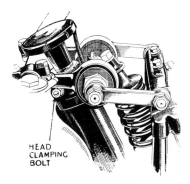

Oil pressure relief valve with ball release   Steering head layout, 1939 Tiger 100

chaincase of streamlined design. It transmitted the power from the 22 tooth (solo) engine drive sprocket and engine drive shaft shock absorber mechanism to the 43 tooth, nine plate (4 corked drive, 5 plain driven) adjustable clutch assembly. A spring-loaded, taper-pointed metering screw provided positive rear chain lubrication from the primary chaincase. Top and lower chainguards were specified, the tyre inflator fitted as standard equipment to pegs attached to the top one.

Frame
A brazed full cradle type with large diameter tapered single down tube front section and bolted-up separate tubular rigid rear frame section.

Forks
Taper tube girder-type forks incorporating a central compression spring and dampers with finger adjustment on the lower bridge.

Fuel Tank
A $3^{1}/_{2}$ (imp) gallon, all steel tank with an integral instrument panel recess, flush mounting the illuminated instrument panel carrying oil gauge, ammeter, switch and 'dash' lamp. Equipped with a quick opening hinged filler cap, all metal 'permanent' Triumph badges, large bore cork insert fuel taps and metal braided flexible petrol pipes.

Oil Tank
All-steel, welded with quick opening filler cap, and incorporating a feed line filter, drain plug and separate vent. Oil capacity – 1 gallon.

Brakes

Front: 7 in diameter Triumph design with aluminium alloy anchor plate incorporating single leading brake shoes and a speedometer drive gearbox. The cast iron ribbed drum was detachable from the wheel hub.

Rear: 7 in diameter with bolt-on cast iron brake drum and separate bolted-on plated 46 tooth drive sprocket. Single leading brake shoes were fitted to the pressed steel rear anchor plate which was provided with spring-loaded knurled finger adjustment at the brake rod operating lever fulcrum pin.

Wheels
Triumph wheels of fabricated steel hub design with 'equal length' chrome-plated spokes and chromium plated rims. (WM2-20 front and WM2-19 rear). Rim centres were painted silver sheen and lined blue.

Tyres
Dunlop 26 x 3.00 in ribbed front, 26 x 3.50 in Speed Universal rear.

Mudguards
Painted front and rear rolled steel 'ribbed' mudguards of adequate width, with streamlined stays, front and rear. The rear guard incorporated a detachable tail piece to facilitate rear wheel removal. Both guards were in silver sheen, with black centre stripe, the front equipped with the Triumph patented design chrome ribbed two-piece front number plate assembly.

Exhaust System
Twin downswept $1^3/4$ in diameter chrome exhaust pipes, clamped at the cylinder head exhaust ports with chrome plated finned exhaust pipe clamps, connected to two separate 'cocktail shaker' (two part-detachable) shaped chrome-plated silencers mounted to the lower rear frame tube lugs. By simply removing three screws on each silencer body, the tail end can be detached, leaving the effective front megaphone section in full operating condition.

Air Filter
Not fitted.

Electrical Equipment
Lucas MN2 6 volt gear-driven manual ignition controlled Magdyno with cut-out and voltage regulator feeding the Lucas 6 volt PUW7E-4 battery. Altette electric horn and an 8 in diameter chrome plated headlamp with main, dip and pilot bulbs. Switch gear and ammeter were contained in a flush fitting rubber-mounted moulded Bakelite instrument panel fitted in a recessed panel within the fuel tank, which also housed the oil pressure gauge and a detachable dash lamp which doubled on 'quick-twist' removal as an extending inspection lamp.

Speedometer
Smiths 120 mph Chronometric type speedometer having three inner circles calibrated in rpm corresponding to the road speeds in top, third and second gears, and fitted with an odometer and trip with re-set facility. Fitted as standard equipment, although specified as an 'extra' (a further alternative extra with five inch dial was also available), it was driven from the front wheel carrying the 58 tooth driving gear. The cable drive box assembly (19 tooth pinion – 26 in. tyre, 18 tooth pinion – 27 in. tyre) was mounted on to the aluminium alloy front brake anchor plate assembly.

Handlebars
Resiliently-mounted 1 in diameter chrome-plated handlebars adjustably clamped to the front fork head clip and fitted with chrome-plated TT-type brake and clutch levers. Clutch lever and magneto control (push forward to retard) together with the dipswitch were fitted to the left bar, with the friction-damped twistgrip, carburettor air control lever and horn push on the right bar. The right bar was swaged down in diameter to accept the Triumph positive click-action friction-damped throttle twist grip.

Saddle
A nose hinged Terry de-luxe soft black top type saddle, with adjustable rear chromed springs was fitted. A rear mudguard-mounted black covered pillion seat and pillion footrests were available as an extra.

Toolbox
The large capacity all steel, rubber-sealed tool box was fitted on the right side of the rear frame section, containing seven spanners in a tool roll.

Finish

Frame:	Black
Forks:	Black
Mudguard – front:	Silver sheen with black central stripe
– rear:	Silver sheen with black central stripe

Fuel tank:	Chromium plated, with silver sheen top and side panels, twin lined in blue (broad inners – narrow outer)
Oil tank:	Black
Switch panel:	Black moulded
Wheels:	Chromed spokes and wheel trims, with silver sheen centre strip, lined in blue

Extras
Rear stop light.
Smiths Chronometric 120 mph speedometer with rpm scale.
or as above with 5 inch dial.
Pillion footrests.
Rear carrier.
26 x 3.50 in Dunlop tyres.
Propstand.
Pillion seat.
Quickly detachable rear wheel.
Straight-through exhaust pipes

1940 Tiger 100 showing the additional front fork check springs

1940 model: Triumph T100 Tiger 100 Twin
Commencing Engine Number: 40-T100 followed by the series number
Model: T100
Associated 'B' range model: 500cc 5T model 'Speed Twin'

Historical Note
New season's models had customarily been announced at the time of the annual International Motor Cycle Show in November, but by that time in 1940, World War 2 had already begun. However, although the 1939 model Tiger 100 had proven to be an exceptional success, the approaching dark clouds of the conflict yet to come had not discouraged a series of listed improvements which were to be introduced in the 1940 range, even whilst the contracts for the supply of machines for the War Department were being geared up. Although never catalogued, they are listed and recorded as under:-

Engine
Full skirted pistons replaced the slipper type. Modifications were made to the lubrication system – to avoid pressure loss. A piston-type oil release valve was fitted, replacing the ball release valve, and

Oil pressure relief valve now with piston

modifications were made to the connecting rod big-ends to provide additional lubrication to the cylinder walls, and better oil flow through the engine.

Primary Transmission

All models were geared one tooth higher on the engine sprocket to provide an improved mileage per gallon. The Tiger 100 was quoted as giving 100 mpg at 40 mph.

Forks

The girder-type front fork main central spring was lightened to provide increased response at the static load position and at the same time twin external check springs were introduced.

Fuel Tank

Now fitted with a metal instrument panel, painted with a crystalline 'crackle' finish, replacing the previous moulded Bakelite version.

Mudguards

Fully valanced front and rear mudguards were offered, together with a rear carrier as an optional extra.

The colour scheme remained exactly as its 1939 predecessor, until displaced by the increasing output of khaki-coloured military models, all to end abruptly in November 1940.

1946 Catalogue photograph, illustrating the new telescopic front fork

1946 model: Triumph T100 Tiger 100 Twin
Commencing Engine Number: 72000
Model: T100 Tiger 100
Associated 'B' range model: 5T Speed Twin

At the re-commencement of post-war production, the Tiger 100 was reintroduced in restricted quantities due to shortages of essential manufacturing materials. Quality was, however, stringently maintained, resulting in limited production and long customer waiting lists. This situation was to be 37 maintained, almost as an unwritten company policy for years to come – as popularity and demand increased.

Engine

1946 saw the reintroduction of the double high camshaft, ohv vertical twin with a bore of 63 mm, and stroke of 80 mm, giving a cubic capacity of 498cc. The engine had a high compression of 7.75:1, Lo-Ex alloy pistons operating within the cast-iron one-piece cylinder barrel, and a one-piece cylinder head. The vertically split crankcase, manufactured in aluminium alloy, contained the three-piece crankshaft

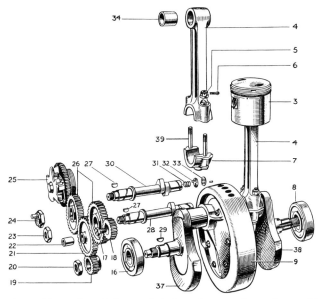

1946 parts catalogue illustration of the crankshaft and connecting rod assembly, showing the method of fixing the white metalled steel end caps to the alloy connecting rods

and flywheel assembly incorporating 'H' section RR56 Hiduminium connecting rods with Babbit metal-lined big-end caps. All the moving parts were highly polished. The valve gear was totally enclosed and positively lubricated from the oil tank return line, via a 'twig' junction pipe to the rocker spindles, the valve mechanism incorporating twin aero quality valve springs. Rocker chamber oil drainage was now achieved via vertical drillways down through the cylinder head, gasket and cylinder barrel, dispensing with the previous oil drain pipes connected to the pushrod cover tubes. Dry sump lubrication was provided by means of the readily accessible twin plunger oil pump within the timing chest, controlled by an oil pressure relief valve in the cover and providing positive oil feed to the crankshaft big ends. The timing chest cover also incorporated an oil pressure feed line banjo take-off point to the tank top panel oil pressure gauge. This year, all completed engines were individually bench tested, stripped, re-assembled and built into motorcycles each supplied with a certified test card.

Gearbox

A Triumph patented four-speed gearbox was fitted with a fully-enclosed positive stop right footchange mechanism, and containing gears and shafts of hardened nickel chrome steel.

Primary Transmission

Transmission was by single row primary $^3/_8$ in pitch primary chain running in a sealed and polished cast aluminium oil bath chain case of streamlined design. Power was transmitted from the 22 tooth (solo) engine drive sprocket and engine drive shaft shock absorber mechanism to the 43 tooth, nine plate (4 corked drive/5 plain driven) adjustable clutch assembly. A spring-loaded, taper-pointed metering screw provided positive rear chain lubrication from the primary chaincase, top and bottom chainguards being fitted, the tyre inflator fitted as standard equipment to pegs attached to the top one.

Frame
A fully brazed lug, tubular-type cradle frame, with large diameter tapered single front down tube. The frame assembly comprised bolted together separate front and rear sections.

Forks
An entirely new post-war Triumph development. Telescopic front forks were introduced with six inches of movement, internal fork springs, hydraulic damping and integral automatic lubrication.

The new post-was telescopic front fork, showing the front brake cable with sliding tube arrangement and knurled finger adjustment

Fuel Tank
Chrome plated 4 (imp) gallon steel tank, with instrument panel recess, and side recesses for special Triumph embossed rubber knee grips. It was equipped with twin large bore cork inserted fuel taps and metal braided flexible petrol pipes. A quick release chrome hinged filler cap was fitted.

Oil Tank
One gallon (imp) capacity all steel welded oil tank fitted with large quick action filler cap, drain plug, accessible filter, a rocker feed pipe take-off and separate vent.

Brakes
Front: 7 in diameter Triumph design single leading shoe drum brake, with aluminium alloy front brake anchor plate and finger adjustment at the anchor plate cable abutment.

39

Rear: 7 in diameter Triumph design single leading shoe
                                         with pressed steel rear anchor plate and provided
                                         with a spring loaded knurled finger adjuster at
                                         the brake rod operating lever fulcrum pin.

Wheels
Of Triumph design, front and rear, with black painted fabricated steel hubs, bolted on cast-iron black
brake drum and separate bolt-on plated drive sprocket with chromium plated rims and spokes. The
rim centres were painted silver sheen and lined in blue.

Tyres
Dunlop Universal tyres were fitted, 26 x 3.25 in front, 26 x 3.50 in rear, as at first specified, later to be
re-designated as 3.25 x 19 in front and 3.50 x 19 in rear.

Mudguards
Painted front and rear rolled steel 'ribbed' mudguards were of generous width, mounted on front and
rear streamlined stays. Finish was in silver sheen with black centre stripe applied to the central raised
strengthening rib, the rear guard having a detachable tail piece to aid rear wheel removal. The front
guard was equipped with a front stand and the Triumph patented design chrome-ribbed two-piece
front number plate assembly.

Exhaust System
Twin downswept chromed exhaust $1^3/4$ in diameter exhaust pipes, clamped at the cylinder head
exhaust ports with chrome plated finned exhaust pipe clamps. Connected to separate parallel
cylindrical chrome-plated silencers with axial entry/exit, mounted direct onto the lower rear frame
tube lugs.

Air Filter
Not fitted.

Electrical Equipment
Lucas gear-driven dynamo 6 volt lighting set with voltage regulator control feeding the Lucas 6 volt
battery, electric horn and the 6 in diameter chromed headlamp with main, dip and pilot bulbs. Switch
gear and ammeter were contained in a flush-fitting rubber-mounted instrument panel fitted in a recess
within the fuel tank top, housing the oil pressure gauge and detachable dash lamp, which doubled on
'quick-twist' removal as an extending inspection lamp. Ignition was provided by either a Lucas K2F or
a BTH KC2 magneto, equipped with a centrifugal auto-advance mechanism.

Speedometer
A Smiths illuminated 120 mph Chronometric speedometer with rpm scale, an odometer and a trip with
reset facility was available as an optional extra, mounted on the front fork top lug. It was cable driven
from the rear wheel speedometer drive gearbox.

Handlebars
Triumph one inch diameter handlebars, adjustably clamped to the front fork top lug, and fitted with
long lever type front brake and clutch levers with cable adjusters. The engine/magneto cut-out button
and dipswitch were fitted to the left bar, with the horn button on the right bar. The right bar was
swaged down in diameter to accept the Triumph quick action friction-damped throttle twist grip.

Saddle
Nose hinged spring de-luxe saddle, with black renewable cover supported on adjustable rear chrome
springs. A rear mudguard mounted waterproof vinyl-covered pillion seat was available as an extra.

Toolbox
A pressed steel tool box with hinged lid and knurled screw fastening was attached to the right side
lower rear frame tube, and was equipped with a complete set of 'good quality' tools, including a tool
roll, clutch centre extractor and grease gun.

Finish

Frame:	Black
Forks:	Black
Mudguards – front:	Silver sheen with black centre stripe
– rear:	Silver sheen with black centre stripe
Fuel tank:	Chromium plated with silver sheen panels – lined out in blue
Oil Tank:	Black
Switch panel:	Matt black – crinkle finish
Wheels:	Chromed spokes and wheel rims, silver sheen centre strip, lined in blue

Extras

Speedometer or:-
Speedometer with rpm 'indicator' on dial
Pillion footrests
Pillion seat

Right side view of the 1947 Tiger 100 now fitted with the new rear wheel incorporating the spring hub

1947 model: Triumph T100 Tiger 100 Twin
Commencing Engine Number: 79046
Model: T100 Tiger 100
Associated 'B' range models: 5T Speed Twin

Engine
As 1946 model. No mention was made this year of individual engine bench testing!

Gearbox
As 1946 model.

Primary Transmission
As 1946 model.

Frame
As 1946 model.

Forks
As 1946 model.

Fuel Tank
As 1946 model.

Oil Tank
As 1946 model.

Brakes
Front and standard rear as 1946 model. The MkI rear Spring Wheel incorporated an 8 inch diameter brake drum and sprocket with single leading shoe rear brake mounted on a combined rear brake anchor plate and long pivoted torque arm.

Wheels
Triumph design wheels were used, front and rear, with black-painted fabricated steel hubs and chrome plated rims and spokes. Rim centres were in silver sheen, lined in blue. The MkI rear Spring Wheel was introduced as an optional extra, having an aluminium alloy hub finished in black, with a black side cover.

Tyres
As 1946 model.

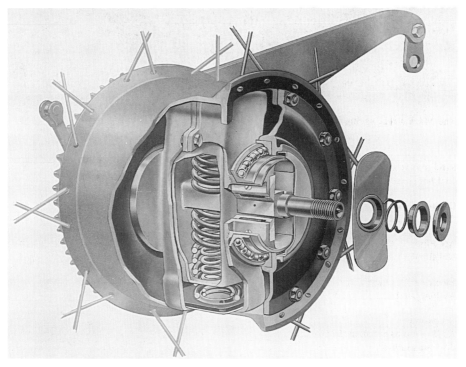

Sectioned illustration of the rear spring wheel showing clearly the internal curved plunger box and suspension springing arrangement

The Mark I rear spring hub and the detachable tail piece on the rear mudguard

Mudguards
As 1946 model.

Exhaust System
As 1946 model.

Air Filter
Not fitted.

Electrical Equipment
As 1946 model.

Speedometer
As 1946 model except in the case of the rear spring hub, where a gearbox-driven auxiliary speedometer drive was utilised.

Handlebars
As 1946 model.

43

Saddle
As 1946 model.

Toolbox
As 1946 model.

Finish
As 1946 model.

Extras
Speedometer, or:-
Speedometer with rpm 'indicator' on dial
Pillion footrests
Pillion seat
Propstand
Spring wheel (Mk1)

Right hand side view of the 1948 Tiger 100, no longer having the rear mudguard detachable tail piece in favour of a 'quickly detachable' section from beneath the saddle

1948 model: Triumph T100 Tiger 100 Twin
Commencing Engine Number: 88782
Model: T100 Tiger 100
Associated 'B' range models: T100 Grand Prix and 5T Speed Twin

Engine
As 1946 model.

Gearbox
As 1946 model.

Primary Transmission
As 1946 model.

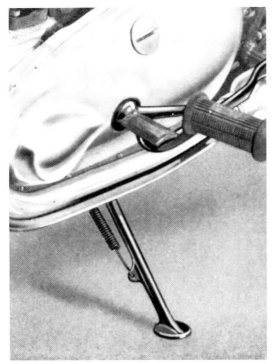

The clamp-on propstand, offered as an extra for 1948

Frame

There was no change made to the front half of the frame for 1948, but the bolt-up tubular brazed lug rigid rear section was modified to accept the new detachable rear mudguard assembly.

Forks

As 1946 model.

Fuel Tank

As 1946 model.

Oil Tank

As 1946 model.

Brakes

As 1946 model but with 1947 MkI Spring Wheel option.

Wheels

As 1946 model but with 1947 MkI Spring Wheel option.

Tyres

Dunlop tyres were fitted, 3.25 x 19 in ribbed front, 3.50 x 19 in Universal rear.

Mudguards

Front mudguard as 1946 model but introducing the Triumph 'one piece' chromed ribbed front number plate which continued unchanged until 1961. A new rear guard was introduced, detachable from a junction beneath the saddle, simplifying rear wheel removal.

45

Illustrating the new rear frame section and detachable rear mudguard arrangement introduced in 1948

Exhaust System
As 1946 model.

Air Filter
Not fitted.

Electrical Equipment
As 1946 model.

Speedometer
No longer supplied as an optional extra. Cable-driven from the rear wheel speedometer drive gearbox on rigid rear wheel models up to No. 19576. Thereafter the gearbox-driven speedometer drive gearbox was specified as standard.

Handlebars
As 1946 model.

Saddle
As 1946 model.

Toolbox
As 1946 model.

Finish
As 1946 model.

Extras
As 1947 model, except that the speedometer was now regarded as a standard fitting (but charged as an extra!)

Left side view of the 1949 Tiger 100, now fitted with front fork nacelle containing the instruments and switches, replacing the tank top instrument panel. The parcel grid is not shown in this illustration but was available as an extra

1949 model: Triumph T100 Tiger 100 Twin
Commencing Engine Number: 100762
Model: T100 Tiger 100
Associated 'B' range models: 5T Speed Twin and T100 Grand Prix

Engine
As 1946 model, but now featuring a new single lipped roller bearing (later in conjunction with a captive chip shield) on the right hand and introducing oil pressure 'tell tale' indicator now incorporated in timing cover oil pressure relief valve. Previous pressure gauge feed point now blocked off.

The oil pressure relief valve incorporated a 'tell-tale' button which protruded, indicating satisfactory oil line pressures

Gearbox
As 1946 model.

Primary Transmission
As 1946 model but now introducing a new type heat-treated engine sprocket (interchangeable).

Frame
Changes were made to the front frame section to accommodate the revised engine torque stay whilst the rear section incorporated integral sidecar attachment points either side and carried amended brackets to mount the new type voltage regulator beneath the saddle. The battery carrier was extended and moved to accommodate the new air filter.

Forks
The unique Triumph Nacelle, designed as an integral instrument panel and headlamp mount surmounting the telescopic front forks, was introduced for 1949. It proved to be the essence of   47

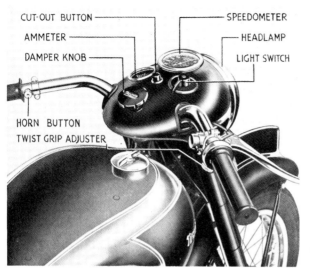

CUT-OUT BUTTON ———————— SPEEDOMETER
AMMETER ———————— HEADLAMP
DAMPER KNOB ———————— LIGHT SWITCH

HORN BUTTON
TWIST GRIP ADJUSTER

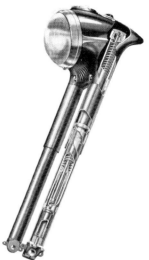

Detailed view of the 1949 nacelle and handlebar layout

Sectioned view of the 1949 telescopic front forks

Triumph design refinement for many years to come. Incorporating the headlamp, speedometer ammeter, lighting switch, cut-out button, steering damper and horn, all the instruments were rubber ring mounted, illuminated, and claimed to be readily accessible. A decorative chromed flash adorned each side. The telescopic front forks continued unchanged, apart from the fitting of the Nacelle.

Fuel Tank
The design of fuel tank continued unchanged apart from the removal of the tank top instrument panel recess in favour of the newly-introduced front fork top instrument nacelle feature. This permitted provision for the fitment of a chrome-plated tank top parcel grid, available as an 'extra'. The Triumph tank badge comprised Triumph in black on a chrome background.

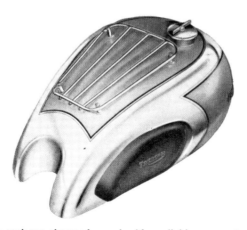

The tank top chromed parcel grid, available as an extra

The air cleaner, introduced in 1949, sandwiched between the oil tank and battery carrier

Oil Tank
48   The oil tank was reshaped to help accommodate the newly-introduced air filter, dropping the chromed

hinged filler cap in favour of a polished, cast aluminium threaded filler cap. Tank capacity was decreased to 6 pints (imp).

Brakes
As 1947 model with spring wheel option.

Wheels
As 1946 model. The Spring Wheel (Mk1) this year introduced hardened slipper pads and shims within the aluminium alloy hub and the integral brake drum and sprocket now incorporated a water deflector shield. The standard rear wheel hub no longer has a rear view speedometer drive facility, deleted at engine number 19576 in favour of the new speedometer drive gearbox mounted externally on the gearbox casing previously introduced for the Mk1 Spring Wheel.

Tyres
As 1948 model.

Mudguards
The forward section of the detachable rear mudguard assembly featured the previous year was reshaped to accommodate the new oil tank and air filter. Otherwise as 1948 model.

Exhaust System
As 1946 model.

Air Filter
An oil-wetted muslin element Vokes air filter to Triumph patented design was now introduced and installed between the battery to the rear of the new oil tank. It was readily detachable and easily cleaned.

Electrical Equipment
A new Lucas gear-driven 6 volt E3L ('L' for 'Long') 60w dynamo was specified, with associated cut-out and voltage regulator feeding the Lucas PUW7E/4 battery. A new electric horn was now accommodated within the headlamp nacelle. The light switch and cut-out button were also moved to the nacelle, which now housed the internally-illuminated ammeter and speedometer, and the steering damper knob. The inspection lamp and oil pressure gauge were discontinued. The ignition system components remained unchanged.

Speedometer
As 1947 model, nacelle-mounted and driven by a gearbox-mounted drive.

Handlebars
The introduction of the front fork nacelle dictated new one inch chrome plated handlebars now located and clamped to the fork top lug by inverted 'U' bolt clamps. Equipped with 'screw-in' concealed horn push and chromed 'long lever' clutch lever and cable adjuster on the left side, the right side had a matching 'long' front combined brake lever and lever abutment with integral dip-switch and cable adjuster.

Saddle
As 1946 model.

Toolbox
As 1946 model.

Finish
As 1946 model.

Extras
As 1947 model, but now including the option of a tank top parcel grid

49

Left side view of the 1950 Tiger 100, showing the new style fuel tank and horizontal styling strips

1950 model: Triumph T100 Tiger 100 Twin
Commencing Engine Number: 100N ('N' suffix)
Model: T100 Tiger 100
Associated 'B' range models: 650cc 6T Thunderbird
                                    500cc 5T Speed Twin
                                    500cc 5T Trophy
                                    500cc Grand Prix

Engine

1950 saw the gradual introduction of small, but significant improvements to the basic specification of the entire machine. A revised cast-iron cylinder barrel and modified cast iron cylinder head no longer featured the vertical rocker cavity drain drillways through the cylinder head, head gasket and cylinder barrel due to the reinstatement of the inlet and exhaust rocker cavity drain pipes connected to the push rod cover tubes. Although the vertically split crankcase in high tensile aluminium alloy continued unchanged, it supported on a heavy duty ball bearing (RH), a new crankshaft assembly incorporating from engine number 713N redesigned connecting rods in RR56 Hiduminium alloy with inverted 'through' con-rod end cap bolts and lower fixing self-lock nuts in lieu of the previous end cap interference fit bolt arrangement with top mounted castellated nut and split pin. The end caps were lined with babbit white metal, bolted-up to the connecting rod and machined in situ. The cylinder head ports and all moving parts were all highly polished. The totally enclosed valve gear continued unchanged.

Gearbox

Quite radical changes were introduced into the 1950 Triumph gearbox, to improve reliability and strength, the most noticeable being the replacement of the separate floating layshaft by a driven layshaft with integral high gear pinion. All the new gear pinions were 'beefed-up' and the box now incorporated an internal layshaft driven speedometer cable drive pinion.

Primary Transmission

The only change in this area was the fitting of a pressed-in hardened bearing outer race to the clutch chain wheel.

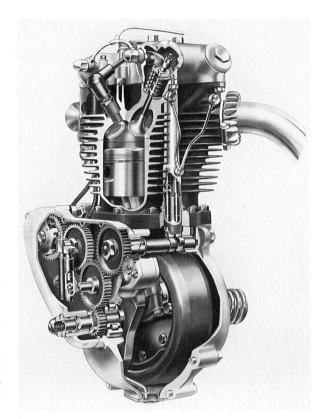

Sectioned view of the 1950 engine unit, showing the cylinder head valve cavity oil drain pipes connecting to the push-rod cover tubes – in favour of the previous oil drain drillways through the cylinder head, gasket and cylinder barrel. This early 1950 engine still utilised the earlier type connecting rods

The new 1950 gearbox incorporating a driven layshaft which provided an integral speedometer cable take-off point

51

Frame

Incorporating the modifications made when the 1949 model was introduced, the rear section now included also a permanent propstand attachment lug. The propstand itself was available as an 'extra', but was fitted as standard to every machine.

Forks

As 1949 model.

Fuel Tank

As 1949 model, but with the addition of the chrome plated tank top parcel grid as standard equipment.

Oil Tank

As 1949 model.

Brakes

As 1947 model with spring wheel option.

Wheels

Front as 1946 model, rear as 1949. The Mk II Spring Wheel became available from engine number 7439 having an aluminium alloy hub, finished in black with black side cover, torque arm and 46 tooth bolt-on integral brake drum and sprocket.

Tyres

As 1948 model.

Mudguards

Front as 1948 model, rear as 1949.

Exhaust System

As 1946 model.

Air Filter

As 1949 model.

Electrical Equipment

As 1949 model.

Speedometer

As 1949 model, but cable now driven from the layshaft drive pinions housed within the gearbox inner cover.

Handlebars

As 1949 model.

Saddle

As 1946 model.

Toolbox

As 1946 model.

Finish

As 1946 model, but petrol tank now in silver sheen with polished alloy styling strips lined in silver sheen, polished chrome nameplate and 'Triumph' picked out in black with a silver background.

Extras

As 1949 model. Mk II Spring Wheel now available.

Left side view of the 1951 Tiger 100, now with the new close pitch fin cylinder barrel and head, Mk II rear spring wheel and featuring the new Twinseat

1951 model: Triumph T100 Tiger 100 Twin
Commencing Engine Number: 100NA ('NA' Suffix)
Model: T100 Tiger 100
Associated 'B' range models: 650cc 6T Thunderbird
                                     500cc 5T Speed Twin
                                     500cc TR5 Trophy

Engine

The pace of introduction of small but significant improvements continued in step with the advance of lubrication and fuel technology, and the increasing demand for sporting performance. The Lo-Ex silicon alloy pistons were now fitted with taper faced second compression piston rings in the new aluminium alloy close-pitch fin cylinder block incorporating cast-in steel liners (E2474). A new matching aluminium alloy close pitch fin cylinder head was equipped with steel screwed in exhaust pipe adaptors. The use of these alloy components reduced the compression ratio slightly to 7.6:1. Later, pressed centrifugally spun cast-iron liners were used – both cylinders were fitted with aluminium alloy tappet guide blocks for this year only. Duralumin push-rods were specified to match the alloy cylinder block expansion rate and Stellite-faced cam followers (tappets) introduced to overcome the prevalent camshaft and tappet wear problems. A new polished flywheel and crankshaft assembly utilised polished versions of the stronger 650cc 6T Thunderbird connecting rods, supported on the previously used heavy duty ball bearing (LH) and single lipped roller bearing (RH). All moving parts and the rocker boxes and inlet ports were highly polished, no change being introduced to the totally enclosed valve gear. Otherwise engine specification as 1950 model.

Gearbox

As 1950 model.

Primary Transmission

The single row $^3/_8$ in pitch primary chain connected the engine drive sprocket to an improved capacity clutch and chainwheel assembly, introduced to accommodate extra cork inserted drive, and driven clutch plates. This necessitated increasing the depth of the clutch centre and lengthening the clutch pressure springs. Specification otherwise as for 1950 model.

The close pitch fin aluminium alloy cylinder block, initially with cast-in liners, and finally with pressed-in centrifugally spun liners

Frame
The 1951 season saw the reintroduction of the earlier 1945/1948 version, to accommodate the newly-introduced engine front torque stays. The rear section was modified to accept heavier duty rear wheel/chain adjusters, and also incorporated integral propstand and sidecar attachment lugs.

Forks
As 1949 model.

Fuel Tank
Now fitted with a bayonet-fitting chrome filler cap and twin lever type taps, the main supply on the right and the reserve on the left. Horizontal aluminium styling strips with alternating alloy and black stripes and tank badges with Triumph painted white on a black ground replaced the 1950 styling.

Oil Tank
A new 6 (imp) pint all steel oil tank of welded design was introduced, the threaded alloy filler cap being replaced by a chrome flat-topped bayonet-fitting type.

Brakes
Front as 1946 model but with revised spoking, rear as 1949 with Spring Wheel option.

Wheels
Front as 1946 model, rear as 1949 with Mk II spring wheel option.

Tyres
As 1948 model.

The Mark II spring wheel, showing the ball races that replaced the original cup-and-cone design

Mudguards
Front as 1948 model, rear as 1949.

Exhaust System
Now incorporating welded-on tags at the forward lower run of the exhaust pipes to accommodate the new chrome brackets attached to the engine front plate lower mounting stud. Otherwise as 1946 model.

Air Filter
No change apart from converting the spares part numbers to Triumph sequence.

Electrical Equipment
Continuing unchanged, apart from the use of a Lucas K2F or BTH KC2 manually-controlled ignition advance magneto, the drive pinion no longer incorporating the centrifugal auto-advance mechanism.

Speedometer
As 1949 model.

Handlebars
As 1949 model, but with the addition of a magneto advance/retard control lever (push to advance) on the left side. High rise handlebars introduced on US models.

Saddle
The saddle was no longer specified for the Tiger 100, being superseded by the new Twinseat – comprising a steel base pan, latex foam interior and black 'Vynide' waterproof cover.

Toolbox
A pressed steel tool box was specified, which incorporated a quick release lid fastening. It was repositioned from the lower rear frame run forward of the pillion footrest and silencer hangar brackets to a new location above the rear frame upper tube, immediately below the Twinseat.

Finish

As 1951 model but with the tank horizontal alloy styling strips now lined black and the 'Triumph' nameplate picked out in white on a black ground.

Extras

The 'Tiger 100' racing kit was catalogued for the first time under CP 100 (8.25:1 compression ratio) and CP 101 (9.5:1), for high octane and petrol benzol mixture alternatives. Kits were not factory fitted to production machines for sale to the public.

Other extras as 1950 model.

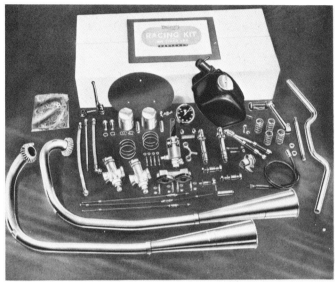

Note. All the above parts are available separately, if required, from the Service Department at usual list prices. Also available are Close Ratio Gears and Racing type alloy Mudguards.

TIGER 100 RACING KIT

Comprises the following :—

(1) PISTONS. Complete with rings. Choice of Compression Ratios—see page 28.
(2) CAMSHAFTS. Two, racing lift type.
(3) VALVE SPRINGS. Four pairs racing type, inner and outer.
(4) CARBURETTERS. Two Amal Type 6 complete with special dual manifold and 'remote' float chamber.
(5) Dual THROTTLE CABLES with junction box.
(6) PETROL PIPES. Two racing type, flexible.
(7) TACHOMETER. Smiths 8000 R.P.M. with cable drive and gearbox.
(8) OIL TANK one gallon capacity with quick release filler cap.
(9) EXHAUST PIPES. Two small diameter with megaphones.
(10) FOOTREST. One folding pattern.
(11) HANDLEBAR. Racing type.
(12) NUMBER PLATE. One regulation oval pattern with brackets.
(13) BRAKE ROD. One short rear.
(14) KICKSTARTER with folding pedal.
(15) JOINTING WASHERS AND GASKETS. One complete set.

▲The original Tiger 100 racing kit

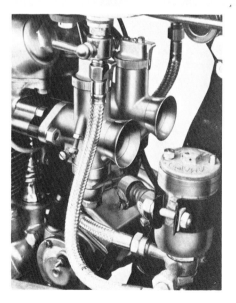

◀ The twin carburettor conversion

Right side view of 1952 Tiger 100. The nacelle now features the pre-focus light unit, and separate pilot light under the nacelle

1952 model: Triumph T100 Tiger 100 Twin
Commencing Engine Number: 15809 NA (NA to 25000, subsequently suffix discontinued)
Model: T100 Tiger 100
Associated 'B' range models: 650cc 6T Thunderbird
500cc 5T Speed Twin
500cc TR5 Trophy

Engine
The close-pitch fin alloy cylinder head and cylinder barrel continued unchanged for 1952. The alloy tappet guide block, although perpetuated on the TR5 Trophy model, now reverted to cast iron material and was used in conjunction with the 1950-type push rod cover tube, with its rocker box oil drain pipe bosses. Otherwise the engine continued to previous specification. An alternative 8:1 compression ratio was available for machines exported to the USA. The Triumph twin plunger oil pump, although of new part number, changed only in respect of the new castellated ball check valve plugs.

Gearbox
As 1950 model.

Primary Transmission
As 1951 model.

Frame
The frame was now modified to feature a split lug within the seat tube to provide direct air filter connection with the carburettor intake. It remained unchanged in all other respects.

Forks
Although the front forks continued unchanged for a further year, the left and right covers and matching nacelle top were redesigned to accommodate the new Lucas MCF 700 7 inch diameter pre-focus headlight unit. As this new equipment incorporated no pilot lamp facility, a new pilot lamp, type 517 was introduced, attached to the fork covers immediately below the headlamp.

57

The 1952 nacelle with additional pilot light, as featured in the catalogue

Fuel Tank
The all steel fuel tank was now constructed with visible raised central seam. The twin lever fuel taps were now connected to the carburettor float bowl by clear plastic feed lines, the metal braided pipes being discontinued.

Oil Tank
Another new 6 (imp) pint oil tank was specified for 1952, redesigned to allow clearance for the new 'D'-shaped air filter, with direct connection through the new special frame lug aperture to the carburettor intake.

Brakes
Front as 1946 model, rear standard wheel now with bolt-on integral brake drum and 46 tooth sprocket. Mk II rear Spring Wheel option.

Wheels
Front as 1951 model, rear now incorporating the new integral 46 tooth brake drum and sprocket.

Tyres
As 1948 model.

Mudguards
Front as 1948 model, rear as 1949.

Exhaust System
As 1951 model.

Air filter
As 1951 model, the air filter now being connected directly through the new open frame lug to the carburettor intake.

Electrical Equipment
A positive earth system was now introduced, along with a new Lucas combined reflector/front lens 'pre-focus' headlamp assembly without a pilot light facility. A neat, separate, Lucas type 517 pilot light slung beneath the headlamp was thus introduced. Specification otherwise unchanged.

Speedometer
As 1949 model.

Handlebars
As 1951 model.

Twinseat
As 1951 model.

Toolbox
As 1951 model.

Finish
As 1951 model.

Extras
The Tiger 100 racing kit continued to be offered, CP100 now having 8.5:1 compression ratio pistons and CP 101 with 9.5:1 alternatives. A new cast iron cylinder barrel was made available for use in conjunction with 12:1 C.R. pistons with alcohol fuel. None of these kits were factory fitted to production machines for sale to the public and were only available through spares channels.
Other extras as 1950 model.

Left side view of 1953 model Tiger 100

1953 model: Triumph T100 Tiger 100 Twin
Commencing Engine Number: 32303
Road Sports Model: T100
Road Racing Model: T100C
Associated 'B' range models: 650cc 6T Thunderbird
                                       500cc 5T Speed Twin
                                       500cc TR5 Trophy

Engine
Three versions of the close-pitch fin alloy engine were produced this year, the first a continuation of the type fitted to the previous season's road-going T100 model, the second for a sporting T100C with racing camshafts and twin Amal carburettors with remote float bowl, and the third a continuation of

the variant used for the 500 TR5 Trophy. The road-going T100 (and TR5) had standard road-going cam form, but the new T100C was fitted with (E3134) racing form cam profiles. At engine number 37560 on the TR5 and road sports T100, new E3275 camshafts were introduced, incorporating 0.010 in opening and closing ramps over 20° of cam movement, in an attempt to quieten the valve operating mechanism. They required 0.010 in tappet clearance and were identified by a 'spoked wheel' mark immediately prior to the crankcase stamped engine identification number. Pistons giving a 'high' compression ratio of 8:1 were used in the US specification T100 variant and the new T100C. In all other respects the engine specification remained unchanged.

Gearbox
Close and wide ratio gear sets, and conversions, were made available, but not supplied on original production assembly. No other changes were made.

Primary Transmission
Now without an engine drive shaft shock absorber, the primary transmission relied of a four vane rubber-damped shock absorber assembly within the clutch centre. Otherwise as 1951 model.

The four vane clutch shock absorber in close detail

Frame
The full cradle type frame continued unchanged and was specified for both the standard road and the new sporting T100C models.

Forks
Identical forks were fitted to both the road and sporting versions, specification as the 1951 model.

Fuel Tank
The steel fuel tank with a visible raised top seam and chrome tank top parcel grid was fitted as standard equipment to both the T100 and T100C models. Clear fuel lines were used for the single carburettor float bowl adaptor on the T100, and metal braided pipes connected to the right side remote float bowl on the T100C model. The fuel tank featured horizontal polished alloy styling strips with alternate alloy and black ribs.

Oil Tank
Two types of oil tank were specified for 1953, a 6 (imp) pint all-steel welded tank for the T100 model and a 1 gallon all-steel welded tank with quick release filler cap for the T100C sports model. Both tanks featured a separate drain plug, accessible filter, rocker feed pipe take-off and vent pipe facility. The T100 racing kit oil tank had an additional built-in anti-froth tower.

Brakes
Front as 1946 model, rear as 1952 model with Spring Wheel option.

Wheels
Front as 1951 model, rear as 1952.

Tyres
As 1946 model.

Mudguards
Front as 1948 model, rear as 1949.

Exhaust System
As 1951 model.

Air Filter
The single carburetter-equipped T100 road model continued to specify the detachable air filter with renewable element, whereas the twin carburetters fitted to the sports T100C model were equipped with intake bell mouths and did not use a filter.

Electrical Equipment
A new type Lucas 525 'Diacon' stop/tail light with wide angle reflective red lens was fitted, otherwise no other changes were made.

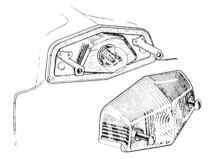

The Lucas model 525 stop-tail lamp

Speedometer
As 1949 model.

Handlebars
One inch diameter chromed handlebars continued to be specified, with an alternative 'high rise' equivalent for the US road machine market. The sports T100C featured sports 'Low-low' handlebars (racing kit bars were also offered in European and US versions).

Twinseat
The Twinseat was fitted to both road and sports verions of the Tiger 100.

Toolbox
Both Tiger 100 and Tiger 100C models specified the pressed steel toolbox.

Finish
As 1951 model.

Extras
This was the last year the boxed Tiger 100 racing conversion kit was offered as the racing camshafts and twin carburettors with remote float bowl had already become standard equipment on the catalogue model T100C – but for this year only.
Other extras as 1950 model.

Left side view of the 1954 Tiger 100, now with the new swinging arm frame, eight inch diameter drum brake with air scoop, 'tear-drop' silencers, two-level Twinseat, and new-type Diacon tail light

1954 model: Triumph T100 Tiger 100 Twin
Commencing Engine Number: 44135
Associated 'B' range models: 650cc T110 Tiger 110
                                         650cc 6T Thunderbird
                                         500cc 5T Speed twin
                                         500cc TR5 Trophy

Engine

Now installed in an entirely new swinging arm frame, the close pitch fin aluminium alloy engine continued, but with significant internal changes. The twin Amal type 76 carburettors with remote float bowl (as last year's T100C model) remained available as an optional extra and the 63 mm x 80 mm bore and stroke ratio continued unchanged, with gear-driven standard road touring ramp camshafts. The newly introduced chrome faced second compression rings were specified for home and general export models, and 8:1 high compression pistons for the US version. The Tiger 100 this year featured a new but unpolished crankshaft and flywheel assembly, with $1^5/8$ inch diameter connecting rod journals and an MS11 ball journal bearing replacing the previous MS10 roller bearing on the RH (timing) side. Highly polished increased section RR56 Hiduminium alloy connecting rods of matching $1^5/8$ inch nominal diameter were also specified, maintaining the Triumph patented system of white metal (micro-babbit) lining within the steel bolt-on end caps, the alloy rod itself providing the upper part of the bearing surface. The new swinging arm frame necessitated a change of engine balance factor, from 68% to 50%, which called for balancing weights of 484 gm. However, with the subsequent urgent need to introduce a form of sludge tube within the new $1^5/8$ in diameter journals which caused an equivalent balance factor drop, the previously used 540 gm balancing weights were re-introduced to restore the final assembly to the desired 50%. (cf. 1956 and the later introduction of B/E shell inserts). The first sludge tubes introduced within the crank journals comprised a single vented tube trapped within the central chamber, located in position with the exit hole facing the centre of rotation by two tight fitting square section 'O' rings held by 'pressed-on' channelled 'bobbins' at each end of the tube. This successful emergency ploy was later superseded by a permanent sludge tube pressed into, and located within, machined counter bores within the cranks themselves. The timing side half of the crankcase was modified to accept the new increased duty ball journal bearing. The totally enclosed valve gear continued unchanged.

The three-piece flywheel assembly was now increased in dimensions and featured $1^5/8$ inch diameter connecting rod journals

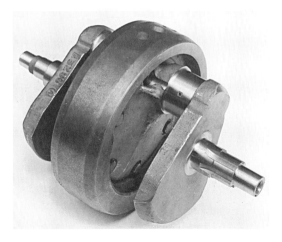

Gearbox

Other than minor changes to the gearbox casing to suit the introduction of the swinging arm frame, the gearbox was unchanged. Close and wide ratio gear sets continued to be available, but were still not fitted on original production assembly.

Primary Transmission

The new swinging arm frame allowed the gearbox to be installed using a shorter 70 link $^3/8$ in pitch primary chain. Rear chain lubrication was continued despite the new shortened primary chaincase by means of the previous metering screw. A top chainguard only was fitted, the tyre inflator being relocated beneath the fuel tank.

Frame

An entirely new single front down tube cradle-type frame with pivoted fork rear suspension made its debut this year. It used 3 position adjustable Girling hydraulic suspension units supported by a new brazed lug tubular rear frame section. Early models had four inch rear suspension unit movement,

The new swinging arm frame for 1954

using 110 lb rate springs, but later models were fitted with 126 lb rate springs and gave 2¹/₂ inches of movement with increased internal rebound damping and making use of bump stops. A black-painted carburettor choke control lever was now installed on the rear frame top stay (LH) immediately beneath the Twinseat, to the rear of the toolbox.

Forks
The Triumph telescopic front forks continued unchanged with the exception of the installation of internal coiled suspension springs that were 20 in in length. The nacelle continued in use, as previously.

Fuel Tank
As 1953 model.

Oil Tank
A new 6 pint (imp) oil tank formed a one-piece unit with the air cleaner, battery and tool box. Fitted on the right side with a bayonet-type chrome filler cap, the oil tank had an accessible filter, drain plug, vent pipe and a rocker feed pipe take-off facility.

The eight inch diameter cast iron brake drum with single leading shoe alloy anchor plate incorporating an air scoop

Brakes
Front:

An entirely new 8 inch diameter single leading shoe drum brake was introduced featuring the readily-identifiable wavy drum side spoke flange. A polished aluminium anchor plate with chrome wire mesh air scoop and associated rear vent completed the new design. Finger adjustment at the anchor plate cable abutment, as previously, was incorporated in the new layout.

Rear:

The previous standard 'rigid' type of rear wheel continued to be offered, but now with revised head angle spoking and journal ball bearings replacing the previous adjustable taper roller bearings. It retained its 7 inch diameter single leading shoe cast-iron bolt-on integral brake drum and 46 tooth sprocket and pressed steel anchor plate.

On this year's swinging arm model, a rear brake anchor plate torque stay was not employed. The previous rigid frame type of anchor plate with its square peg sliding location within the left fork end was used instead. An entirely new quickly-detachable rear wheel was employed, utilising a splined 'fixed position' 7 inch diameter brake drum and a 46 tooth sprocket assembly which allowed, with simple wheel spindle detachment, removal of the complete rear wheel without need to slacken, uncouple, or detach the rear drive chain. This new wheel also carried the pressed steel anchor plate featuring the squared peg sliding location within the channelled left fork end, adjustment remained unaffected.

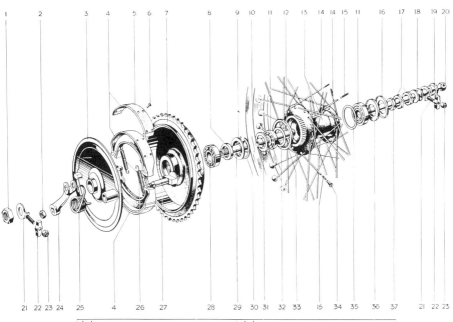

Index No.	Description.	Index No.	Description.
1	Nut, L.H. side sleeve.	19	Collar, spindle.
2	Nut, cam lever.	20	Spindle.
3	Plate, anchor.	21	Adjuster, chain.
4	Shoe c/w lining.	22	End plate, adjuster.
5	Lining, shoe.	23	Nut.
6	Rivet, lining.	24	Lever, brake cam.
7	Brake drum and sprocket.	25	Spring, cam lever return.
8	Felt washer.	26	Spring, shoe return.
9	Retainer, brake drum bearing.	27	Cam, brake operating.
10	Rim, wheel.	28	Bearing, brake drum.
11	Bearing, taper roller.	29	Sleeve, brake drum.
12	Sleeve, bearing.	30	Circlip, bearing retaining.
13	Hub.	31	Cap, dust.
14	Spoke, 76° head.	32	Ring, bearing backing.
15	Spoke, 100° head.	33	Seal, hub to drum dust.
16	Cap, dust.	34	Nipple, spoke.
17	Locknut, bearing.	35	Ring, bearing backing.
18	Collar, spindle distance.	36	Felt washer.
		37	Distance piece, R.H. bearing.

Details of the new quickly detachable rear wheel; note the 'peg' location on the anchor plate   65

Wheels

The front wheel remained unchanged, but in the case of the newly-introduced quickly detachable rear wheel, a splined hub integrated with matching splines within the independently-mounted cast-iron rear brake drum and 46 tooth sprocket assembly. Although the previous rigid rear wheel had adjustable taper roller bearings, they were now changed to ball journal bearings, whereas the new QD (quickly detachable) wheel was introduced with taper roller bearings, within the hub. On all wheels the rim centre was now polished chrome, being no longer painted and lined.

Tyres

As 1946 model.

Mudguards

Front as 1948 model, rear an entirely new mudguard incorporating side valances.

Exhaust System

New chrome plated twin downswept $1^3/4$ inch diameter exhaust pipes with chromed finned exhaust pipe clamps at the cylinder head, braced at the front engine plates. Connected to new chrome-plated axial entry/exit tapering, 'tear-drop' silencers, which were now attached to the rear frame pillion footrest support bracket.

Air Filter

A Vokes 'D' type air filter, with detachable side cover and replaceable concertina element, was located within the 'streamstyle' one-piece oil tank and tool box assembly. A rubber hose connected it in the case of the single carburettor models only. Twin carburettor models had only carburettor bell mouths and no filter.

Electrical Equipment

A New Lucas RB 107 cut out and voltage regulator was fitted, and a Lucas 6 volt 12 ampere hour PU7E-9 battery. The stop/tail light was a Lucas type 525 'Diacon' with a 31437A stop lamp switch, to be replaced by 31383 at engine number 51200. The BTH manually-operated K2C magneto alternative was now discontinued.

Speedometer

As 1950 model.

Handlebars

Home as 1949 model, US as 1950.

Twinseat

A new two-level Twinseat was introduced, with pressed steel base, latex foam interior and covered in black water-proof Vynide, with white piping.

Toolbox

Now part of the one-piece 'streamstyled' mid-frame feature, the pressed steel toolbox unit on the left side of the machine located the air filter, contained the battery and provided adequate accommodation for the tool kit, which now included 14 spanners, a tyre lever, grease gun and clutch key and the reinstated clutch centre extractor.

Finish

Frame	Black
Forks	Black
Mudguard – front	Shell blue sheen with black central stripe lined white.
– rear	Shell blue sheen with black central stripe lined white.

Fuel tank	Shell blue sheen with polished alloy horizontal styling strips, lined black. Polished chrome nameplate with 'Triumph' picked out in white on black background.
Oil tank	Black
Toolbox	Black
Wheels	Black hubs, dull plated spokes, polished chrome rims.

Extras

As 1950 model but including in addition:

Quickly detachable rear wheel

Twin carburettors

A racing kit, although advertised in the 1954 sales catalogue, was never made available, even as separate individual spare parts, and certainly no longer packed in the 'strong container' as indicated! By now, most of the racing fraternity were fabricating their own conversion components for racing – tailored to their own needs, from the pre-swinging arm racing kits.

Left side view of the 1955 Tiger 100, now fitted with rear brake plate torque stay, Type 376 carburettor, front brake drum without 'wavy rim' (despite what the photograph illustrates!) and the new Type 564 tail lamp

1955 model: Triumph T100 Tiger 100 Twin
Commencing Engine Number: 56700
Associated 'B' range models: 650cc T110 Tiger 110
                                                 650cc 6T Thunderbird
                                                 500cc 5T Speed Twin
                                                 500cc TR5 Trophy

Engine

Continuing into the 1955 season, the 'alloy' engine remained unchanged, apart from the 7.6:1 compression ratio Lo-Ex silicon alloy pistons being dropped in favour of the 8:1 higher compression versions utilised previously only for the US market. Single carburettor models now specified the new Amal 376 Monobloc carburettor, whilst twin Amal carburettors with remote float bowl remained as an optional extra. The crankshaft introduced last year was now modified to accept the permanent internal sludge tube, and was supported on two MS11 ball journal bearings. The totally enclosed valve gear continued unchanged too.

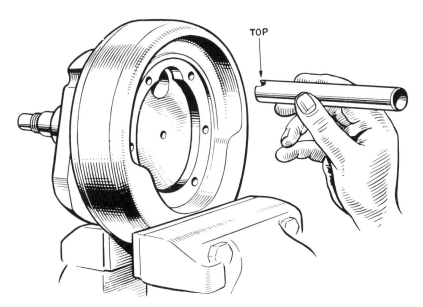

Illustrating the new 1⅝ inch diameter journal crankshaft introduced on the 1954 models, now fitted with the permanent sludge tube

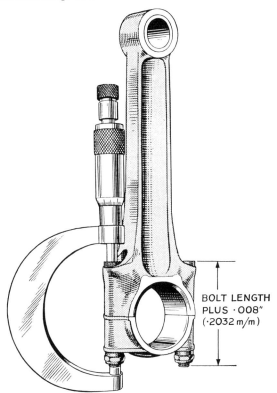

BOLT LENGTH
PLUS ·008"
(·2032 m/m)

The 1954/5 con-rod with white metalled steel end cap bolted to the RR56 hiduminium alloy connecting rod

Gearbox
The gearbox continued unchanged apart from the re-introduction of the pre-war camplate locating plunger to provide more positive location.

Primary Transmission
As 1954 model.

Frame
Improvements to the swinging arm frame introduced last year comprised the incorporation of a lower sidecar fixing lug at the base of the front section seat down tube, and the introduction of a rear brake plate torque arm forward fixing point on the rear swinging arm. A more 'get-attable' propstand was also fitted.

Forks
The Triumph telescopic front forks had the fork crown and stem pinch bolts increased in size to $3/8$ in to improve overall stiffness, and therefore directional stability. No other changes in specification were made.

Fuel Tank
Both the standard 4 (imp) gallon (visible top seam) home and general export, and the newly introduced, but previously standard specification on the TR5 model – seamless 3.6 (US) gallon fuel tanks were of 'streamlined' all-steel welded construction, with bayonet-fitting type chrome filler cap, and chrome tank top parcel grid. The lever type fuel taps (main supply – right, reserve left) connected via clear fuel lines to the single new type Amal Monocloc carburettor on the single carburettor models, and to the remote left side float bowl on the twin Type 76 Amal carburettors, when fitted as an optional extra. The fuel tank styling retained the horizontal polished alloy styling strips with alternate alloy and black ribs and the tank nameplates of polished chrome.

Oil Tank
The 6 (imp) pint oil tank introduced the previous year was modified in construction to overcome an inner wall cracking problem initiated by stresses in manufacture. No other changes were made.

Brakes

Front:	As 1954 model but now modified to provide a constant diameter spoke flange, dispensing with last year's 'wavy' feature which was prone to fracture across the waves.
Rear:	Although a new part number applied to the 1955 rear wheel assembly, the only change was the deletion of the square peg in the anchor plate in favour of a threaded stud to accept the new rear torque arm. Apart from the incorporation of
Quickly detachable:	the new brake torque stay locating stud in the anchor plate, no other changes were made to the independently mounted QD rear wheel assembly.

Wheels
As 1954 model.

Tyres
As 1946 model.

Mudguards
Front as 1948 model, rear as 1954.

Exhaust System
As 1954 model, with the addition of chrome bracing stays from the base of the frame down tube bottom lug to each silencer entry clip.

Air Filter

Other than a minor change to the body of the air filter to match the associated constructional change in the 1955 oil tank, the Vokes 'D' type air filter continued, rubber hose-connected to the carburettor on single carburettor models only.

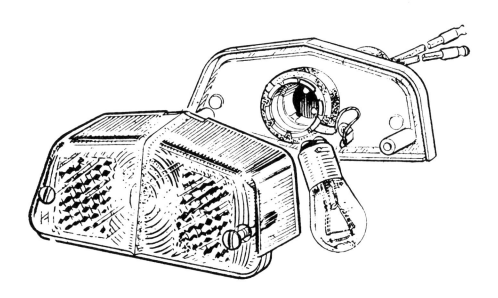

The Lucas model 564 stop-tail lamp incorporating reflex reflectors

Electrical Equipment

A new style Lucas type 564 stop/tail lamp was now fitted incorporating integral reflector surfaces, and was operated by a Lucas type 22B stop lamp switch, otherwise as 1954 model.

Speedometer

As 1950 model.

Handlebars

Home and General Export as 1949, US as 1951.

Twinseat

As 1954 model.

Toolbox

As 1954 model, apart from the toolbox cover, which was of the screw-on type. It replaced the previous 'Dzus' push/turn central fixing design.

Finish

As 1954 model.

Extras

The previously advertised racing kit was now offered in the 1955 sales catalogue as "racing conversion parts available" but none were actually available – only a continuation of the previous "pre-swinging arm" parts – for adaption to the swinging arm application by the purchasers themselves. Other extras as 1954 model.

Left side view of 1956 Tiger 100, no longer with the pilot lamp beneath the nacelle

1956 model: Triumph T100 Tiger 100 Twin
Commencing Engine Number: 70930
(This series ended at 82799 and recommenced with Prefix 'O' at 0100)
Associated 'B' range models: 650cc T110 Tiger 110
                                      650cc TR6 Trophy
                                      650cc 6T Thunderbird
                                      500cc 5T Speed Twin
                                      500cc TR5 Trophy

Engine

Modifications to the close pitch fin alloy engine comprised a reduction in the depth of the cylinder barrel liner spigot (at 70930) from $3/16$ in to $1/8$ in protrusion, with a corresponding reduction in the spigot bore depth into the cylinder head to improve the combustion sphere. Cylinders and heads should therefore always be used as matched pairs. The RR56 Hiduminium alloy connecting rods with forged steel end caps, now incorporated Vandervell steel-backed babbit metal shell bearing inserts.

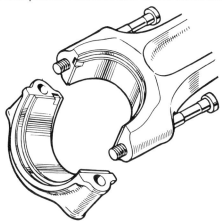

The 1956 con-rod with VP3 steel-backed big-end liners

Introduction of the Vandervell inserts into the connecting rods necessitated a larger big-end eye to accept the new shell bearings. This increased the weight of the rods and made it necessary to use 595 gm balance weights to maintain the 50% balance factor.

The new assembly was supported within the crankcase by two MS11 ball journal bearings. The totally enclosed valve gear continued unchanged.

Gearbox
Only one change was made to the gearbox for 1956, the substitution of sintered bronze layshaft bushes to replace those of phosphor bronze used previously, to aid lubrication.

Primary Transmission
Five newly introduced multi Neo-Langite faced clutch drive plates in conjunction with six new plain driven plates were fitted within the clutch chainwheel assembly.

Frame
The only amendment to the frame for the 1956 season was a modification to the headstock, to replace the 22 x $^3/_{16}$ in ball top steering head race by the 20 x $^1/_4$ inch ball race used also in the bottom position. The rear frame section and swinging fork continued unaltered, although at engine number 74609 a revised rear suspension unit with 100 lb rate springs, 10 lb bleed and 1$^{11}/_{32}$ inch bump stops was introduced.

Forks
No change was made to last year's front fork for 1956.

Fuel Tank
The visible top seams on both the 4 (imp) gallon home and general export, and 3.6 (US) gallon (and TR5) fuel tanks were now trimmed with a neat chromed centre styling band, and fitted with a new two-rung parcel grid replacing the previous 3 rung type. The tanks continued to portray the horizontal polished alloy styling strips with the alternate alloy and black ribs.

Oil Tank
As 1955 model, but in the service literature the realistic capacity of 5 (imp) pints was now quoted in place of the sales-catalogued 6 pints.

Brakes
As 1955 model.

Wheels
As 1954 model.

Tyres
As 1946 model.

Mudguards
Front as 1948 model, rear as 1954.

Exhaust System
As 1954 model.

Air Filter
As 1955 model.

Electrical Equipment
As 1955 model.

Speedometer
As 1950 model.

Handlebars
This year saw only the deletion of the threaded integral horn push in favour of a Lucas chromed combined dip-switch and horn push fixed to the left clutch lever bracket clamp.

Twinseat
As 1954 model.

Toolbox
As 1955 model.

Finish
As 1954 model.

Extras
The 1956 Sales Catalogue advertised racing conversion parts as 'available'. Other extras as 1954 model.

Right side view of the 1957 Tiger 100, now with 'Easy-Lift' centre stand, 'absorption' type silencers and 'mouth-organ' type tank badges

1957 model: Triumph T100 Tiger 100 Twin
Commencing Engine Number: 0945

Associated 'B' Range models: 650cc T110 Tiger 110
  650cc TR6 Trophy
  650cc 6T Thunderbird
  500cc 5T Speed Twin
  500cc TR5 Trophy

Engine
A new 'optional extra' twin carburettor splayed port aluminium cylinder head brought with it the introduction of other associated specification changes. Whereas the single carburettor engine continued unchanged the twin carburettor version with its HDA. 'Delta' cylinder head had increased diameter inlet valves, 9:1 compression ratio pistons, racing (E3134) camshafts and associated 'R' tappets (cam followers), racing interference fit valve spring inners and outers, bronze valve guides and

73

Left-side view of the 1957 Tiger 100

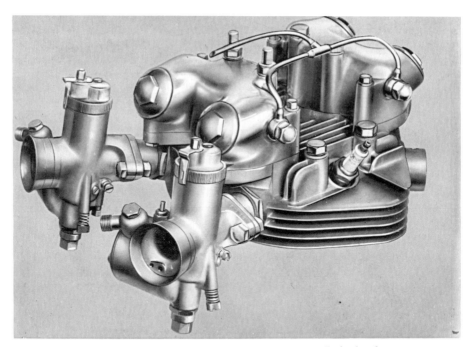

The 1957 optional extra – a twin carburettor HDA Delta alloy cylinder head

no air filters! The chromed second piston ring was dropped, the tapered version being reinstated to re-establish satisfactory oil control The totally enclosed valve gear continued unchanged, except that in the case of the newly-introduced splayed port head, the valve chamber pockets were designed to allow oil drainage direct into the push rod cover tubes, thus obviating the need for the external drain pipes. On single carburettor models ignition continued by Lucas manual control magneto. In other respects the engine specification remained unchanged.

The new twin carburettor head fitted to the close pitch fin alloy cylinder barrel

The original rear suspension units introduced in 1954 with top and bottom eyes fitted with rubber bush and sleeves ▼

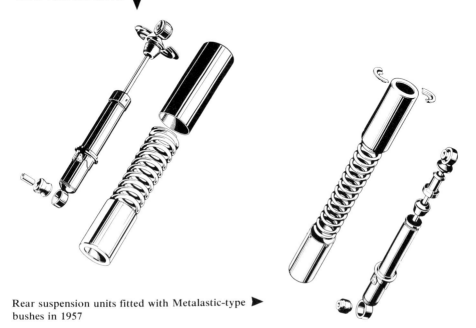

Rear suspension units fitted with Metalastic-type ▶
bushes in 1957

Gearbox

Only one change was made to the gearbox components for 1957, that of extending the mainshaft high gear bush through the primary chaincase oil retainer plate to divert any oil transfer from the mainshaft high gear bush directly into the primary chaincase.

Primary Transmission

The chaincase oil retainer plate (disc) was now of larger bore diameter to accommodate the new high gear extended bush, otherwise the specification remained that of the 1956 model.

Frame

Changes were made to the swinging arm to accept a new rear chainguard, now hinged on a new bracket at the front, and independently bolted-up at the rear in place of utilising the rear suspension unit lower clamp bolt. The 'Easy-Lift' centre stand was introduced, with provision to accommodate the increased stroke rear suspension units (at engine number 08563), now incorporating 110 lb springs, three inch movement with one inch bump stops, 10 lb bleed and for the first time (thereby eliminating road shock transmission to the base valves and consequent loss of damping – and hence Triumph 'weave') Metalastic rubber-bonded upper and lower mounting bushes were incorporated.

Forks

Detailed but important changes were introduced on the 1957 model comprising bolt-up outer member wheel spindle caps to increase the rigidity of the forks, and the use of an induction-brazed mudguard centre stay and brake anchor plate mounting brackets. The latter replaced the previous wrap-round clamps.

Fuel Tank

The fuel tank now featured revised pommel fittings, to accommodate the new style 'mouth-organ' tank badges and associated horizontal chromed styling strips. The Triumph name was now integral, and

76   The 'mouth-organ' (as it was dubbed) type tank badge introduced in 1957.

'cast-in' with a finish of polished chrome and white paint on a black background. Clear plastic fuel lines were now used for the twin Monobloc carburettors when fitted to the 'Delta' splayed inlet port cylinder head.

Oil Tank
As 1955 model.

Brakes

Front:	The 8 in diameter brake was fitted with a revised polished aluminium alloy anchor plate and chromed mesh air scoop and associated rear vent, externally identical to previous years (which could be utilised for previous models with suitable spacer), but with brazed fork lugs on the bottom outer members. The front brake cable abutment that provided ready finger adjustment at the lower end was now transferred to the brake shoe fulcrum pin, retaining the outer cable sliding tube feature.
Rear:	As 1955 model.

Wheels
The front hub design was now changed to accommodate the new clamp-up fixed spindle and circlip located left side bearing. The bolt-on integral brake drum and sprocket at the rear was amended this year to incorporate 8/10 G butted spokes – to overcome the previous 9 gauge breakage problems – as was the splined hub and sprocket arrangement in the case of the QD rear wheel.

Tyres
As 1946 model.

Mudguards
Front as 1948 model, rear as 1954.

Exhaust System
The sway bracing stays from the base of the frame down tube bottom lug to each silencer entry clip were strengthened in section as were the silencer nose clips and the mounting brackets of the axial entry/exit tapering 'tear-drop' absorption-type silencers.

Air Filter
As 1955 model.

Electrical Equipment
As 1955 model.

Speedometer
As 1950 model.

Handlebars
Twin carburettor models were now fitted with the manual magneto control located on the left side. (The clutch and front brake lever abutments were fitted with knurled, cam-action, cable adjusters).

Twinseat
As 1954 model.

Toolbox
As 1955 model.

Finish	UK standard finish	Optional and Export
Frame	Black	Black
Forks & nacelle	Black	Black
Mudguard – front	Crystal grey with black central stripe lined white	Ivory with Meriden blue central stripe lined black
– rear	Crystal grey with black central stripe lined white	Ivory with Meriden blue central stripe lined black
Fuel tank	Crystal grey with polished chrome single horizontal trim band either side of the new 'mouth-organ' chrome tank badge. Polished chrome nameplate with 'Triumph' picked out in white on black ground	Ivory tank top half, Meriden blue lower with black dividing line, polished chrome single horizontal trim band either side of the new 'mouth-organ' chrome tank badge. Polished chrome nameplate with 'Triumph' picked out in white on black background.
Oil tank	Black	Black
Toolbox	Black	Black
Wheels	Black hubs, dull plated spokes with polished chrome rims.	Black hubs, dull plated spokes with polished chrome rims.

Extras
The 1957 catalogue stated that racing conversion parts were available. Other extras as 1954 model, with the addition of a two-tone ivory/Meriden blue finish.

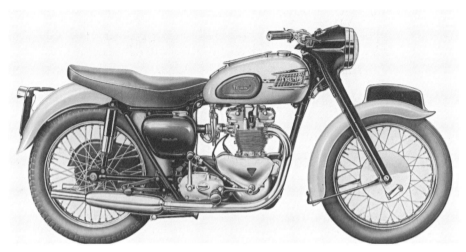

Right side view of the 1958 Tiger 100, with the 'one-piece' valanced rear mudguard, new type valanced front guard, eight inch front drum brake, one and a half inch diameter exhaust pipes, anti-theft steering lock and 'Slickshift' gearchange

1958 model: Triumph T100 Tiger 100 Twin
Commencing Engine Number: 011116
Associated 'B' range models: 650cc T110 Tiger 110
                                          650cc TR6 Trophy
                                          650cc 6T Thunderbird
                                          500cc 5T Speed Twin
                                          500cc TR5 Trophy

Engine
The only change was to fit the left side of the crankcase with an engine mainshaft oil seal in conjunction with a revised ground engine drive sprocket, to eliminate oil transfer and improve engine breather depression.

Engine mainshaft sprocket oil seal and ground sprocket

Gearbox
A new feature coined 'Slickshift' was introduced, providing simultaneous over-riding clutch action when using the gearchange pedal for changing gear. It was achieved by the introduction of a footchange quadrant ramp acting on a roller thrust pin fixed to the clutch operating lever operating arm (now of necessity incorporating a split pin to stop the cable jumping out!) A highly acclaimed feature more often removed by the owner of a T100 than retained! The gearbox outer cover was amended visibly to accept the now vertical clutch operating lever shaft, and incorporate an oval, chromed, screwed-on inspection cover, in place of the previous threaded oil filler cap. A black rubber sleeve was fitted between the kickstart pedal and gearbox outer cover to minimise oil weepage.

Primary Transmission
The 22 tooth engine sprocket was now machined to be accepted by the new crankcase oil seal. No other changes were made.

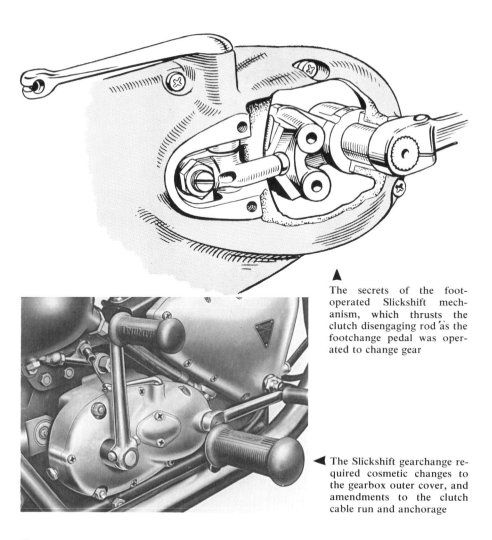

▲ The secrets of the foot-operated Slickshift mechanism, which thrusts the clutch disengaging rod as the footchange pedal was operated to change gear

◀ The Slickshift gearchange required cosmetic changes to the gearbox outer cover, and amendments to the clutch cable run and anchorage

Frame
Introduction of an anti-theft steering head lock amended the part number of the front frame section, the rear swinging arm and rear frame section, together with the centre and propstands remaining unchanged.

Forks
Changes were made to the nacelle top cover to provide an easier run for the control cables by incorporating additional grommet-protected access hole piercing just forward of the handlebars. The fork stem now carried a vertical machined groove to accept the body of the newly introduced frame headlug steering lock. The forks were now equipped with new outer sliding members with more substantial brazed-on lugs to support a new valanced front mudguard central bridge piece, having dispensed altogether with the previous front stays.

Fuel Tank
As 1957 model.

Oil Tank
Although retaining the same part number, the filler cap was moved to a more convenient upright position to avoid fouling the rider's leg when kickstarting.

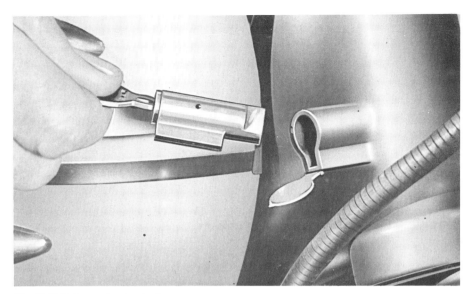

The 1958 Neiman steering lock

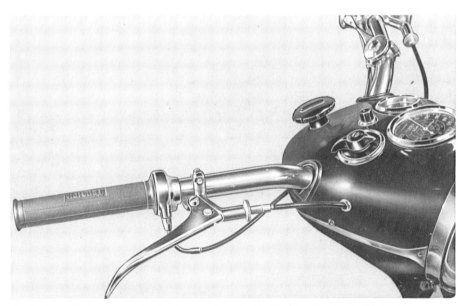

Revised nacelle top cover piercing to provide a neater (and more manageable) cable run

Brakes

Front:
The previous front hub and brake drum assembly was now replaced by an 8 inch diameter cast iron, single leading shoe, full-width finned hub, with polished aluminium anchor plate and chrome plated radially-fluted cover plate.

Rear:
Standard and QD as 1955 model.

Wheels

A new eight inch diameter cast-iron full-width finned hub comprised two dished circular steel pressings riveted to the central internal hub flange, the inner bore diameters being induction brazed to the machined central hub tube. A circlip restrained the wheel bearing and dust cover on the left side and a lockring clamped the locating bearing on the right side. Forty 8/10 gauge straight butted spokes were specified. The rear hub remained unchanged.

Tyres

As 1946 model.

Mudguards

The rear mudguard no longer had the added-on side valances in favour of a new but visually similar deeper drawn single piece replacement. The new valanced front guard, now with a central stiffening bridge piece to mount to the new front fork outer members, dispensed with the front mounting stays but retained the rear stay which also functioned as the front stand, when required. The Triumph chrome ribbed front number plate continued to be specified and fitted.

Exhaust System

Twin downswept chrome plated exhaust pipes of $1^1/_2$ in diameter were now introduced, with chromed finned exhaust pipe clamps at the cylinder head and chromed bracing straps to the front engine plate lower stud. New sway-bracing stays were required for the new axial chrome plated axial entry/exit "straight through" tear-drop silencers used in conjunction with the new $1^1/_2$ in diameter exhaust pipes.

Air Filter

As 1955 model.

Electrical Equipment

The UK and General Export single carburettor models continued using the Lucas K2F manually

82   **The first chromed 'fluted' cover to the eight inch diameter full width hub**

controlled gear driven magneto, whereas some export, and all US models, were fitted with auto-advance magnetos. In other respects the electrical equipment was similar to that specified for the 1955 model.

Speedometer
As 1950 model.

Handlebars
As 1957 model.

Twinseat
As 1954 model.

Toolbox
As 1955 model.

Finish	UK Standard Finish	Optional & Export Finish
Frame:	Black	Black
Forks & Nacelle	Black	Black
Mudguards – front	Crystal grey with black central stripe lined white	Ivory with black central stripe lined white
– rear	Crystal grey with black central stripe lined white	Ivory with black central stripe lined white
Fuel Tank	Crystal grey with polished chrome single horizontal trim band either side of the chrome 'mouth-organ' tank badge. Polished chrome nameplate 'Triumph' picked out in white on black ground.	Black tank top half with ivory lower and white dividing line. Polished chrome single horizontal trim band either side of the chrome 'mouth-organ' tank badge. Polished nameplate 'Triumph' picked out in white on black ground.
Oil Tank	Black	Black
Tool Box	Black	Black
Wheels	Black hubs, dull plated spokes with polished chrome rims	Black hubs, dull plated spokes with polished chrome rims

Extras
The 1958 catalogue continued to list 'racing conversion parts available'. Other extras as 1954 model, with addition of front fork steering lock.

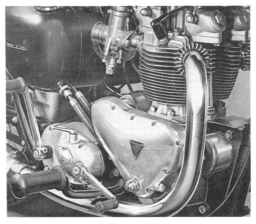

The new 1¹/₂ inch diameter exhaust pipes

1959 Tiger 100, right side view. Some say the last of the 'real' Tiger 100s but certainly the last of the close pitch fin pre-unit engines with separate gearbox, and the last of the heavyweight long strokers!

1959 model: Triumph T100 Tiger 100 Twin
Commencing Engine Number: 020076
Associated 'B' range models: 650cc T120 Bonneville
                                650cc T110 Tiger 110
                                650cc TR6 Trophy
                                650cc 6T Thunderbird

Engine

This was to prove the last year of the 63 mm x 80 mm bore and stroke alloy Tiger 100 engine, although the associated 650cc variants continued forward from this point, with the introduction of the twin carburettor T120 'Bonneville' model. The last of the "alloy" Tigers were still produced in two versions, the standard single carburettor model and the twin carburettor version. An indirect benefit from the introduction this year of the new 650cc 'Bonneville' was a 500cc variant of the new $1^5/8$ in diameter journal one-piece forged crankshaft assembly with bolt-on central cast-iron flywheel. The 500cc version had straight sided crank cheeks, a $2^1/4$ in wide flywheel and a balance factor of 50% with the recently-introduced Vandervell connecting rod shell bearing inserts. The new crankshaft assembly continued to be supported identically within the unchanged crankcase halves.

Gearbox

The gearbox continued unchanged for a further year apart from the introduction of a two level stand pipe and drain plug. 'Slickshift' addition to the gearchange operation continued.

The one-piece forged crankshaft assembly (straight sided) with thread-over bolt-on cast iron flywheel

Primary Transmission
As 1958 model.

Frame
As 1958 model.

Forks
As 1958 model.

Fuel Tank
As 1958 model.

Oil Tank
As 1957 model.

Brakes
As 1958 model.

Wheels
As 1958 model except in the case of the QD wheel fitted to US models which used a WM3 x 18 standard wheel rim for the first time.

Tyres
As 1946 model, but 4.00 x 18 in Dunlop Universal fitted to US models.

Mudguards
As 1958 model. US models were now fitted with a narrow sports-type front 'fender' with tubular centre, front and rear stays. The Triumph chromed ribbed front number plate continued to be specified and fitted.

Exhaust System
As 1958 model but the earlier internally baffled 'absorption' axial entry/exit 'tear drop' silencers were reintroduced.

Air Filter
As 1955 model.

Electrical Equipment
As 1957 model.

Speedometer
As 1950 model.

Handlebars
As 1957 model.

Twinseat
The two-level Twinseat continued for 1959. A Twinseat safety strap was introduced for passenger safety (to comply with California legislation) on West Coast models.

Toolbox
As 1955 model.

Finish
Home and General Export models as 1958, but US models still in ivory and black, lined white, this year reversed with the fuel tank having an ivory top half and a black lower half.

Extras
The 1959 catalogue continued to list 'racing conversion parts available'. Other extras as 1958 model.   85

PART FOUR

1960-1974
Unit Construction
T100
Year-by-Year
model description

PART TWO
THE UNIT-CONSTRUCTION TIGER 100

The new unit-construction Tiger 100 differed in almost every respect from its predecessor and used very few of the earlier model's components in its construction. Although the smaller 150cc and 200cc Terrier and Tiger Cub single cylinder models had already re-introduced the integral engine, gearbox and transmission unit concept in the post-war period, the 350/500cc twin cylinder range of models, to be known henceforth as the 'C' range, was an entirely new Triumph development.

At this point of introduction to the story of the continuing development of the Tiger 100 model, the first of the 'C' range models to be introduced into service was the 350cc Twenty One of 1957. Its name commemorated both the twenty-first year of successful operation of the Triumph Engineering Company Limited, and at the same time signified to the US user its twenty-one cubic inch engine capacity. In 1958 the designation changed to that of 3TA Model Twenty One, and by 1959 a 500cc variant was revealed, the 5TA, to perpetuate the now famous Speed Twin name.

It was therefore logical that since the earlier pre-unit 5T Speed Twin had given way to the new unit-construction 5TA Speed Twin, its original pre-unit stablemate, the Tiger 100, should, in 1960, give way to its natural successor, the new T100A model. It was described in the 1960 Triumph sales catalogue as 'something really new in the way of quick 500s.'

This completely new T100A model weighed only 350 lbs, some 50 lbs lighter than its 'B' range predecessor, the heavier pre-unit models now being continued only in the 650cc category – ultimately itself to be replaced by similar unit construction versions in 1963, to give rise to the legendary Trophy and Bonneville models of the 1970s and 80s. Details describing the new T100A model will, in consequence, be confined to a description of the basic differences from the previous year's 350cc 3TA 'C' range Twenty One model and the recently introduced unit-construction 500cc 5TA Speed Twin.

The 1960 unit-construction T100A Tiger 100 model

1960 model: Unit-construction T100A Tiger 100 model

Technical Data

Engine

Bore:	69 mm
Stroke:	65.5 mm
Cylinder capacity:	490cc
Compression ratio:	9:1
Tappet clearance (cold):	
Inlet:	0.010 in
Exhaust:	0.010 in
Valve timing @ 0.020 in:	27° BTC
	48° ABC
	48° BBC
	27° ATC
Ignition type:	Energy Transfer
Ignition setting (fully advanced):	37° BTDC
BHP @ rpm:	32 @ 7000

Gearbox

	Overall Ratio	Internal Ratio
Top:	4.8	1.0
Third:	5.69	1.19
Second:	8.44	1.76
First:	11.66	2.43

Engine rpm @ 10 mph in top gear:	670
Engine sprocket:	26 teeth
Clutch sprocket:	58 teeth
Gearbox sprocket:	20 teeth
Rear wheel sprocket:	43 teeth

Carburettor

Type:	Amal 375/35
Choke size:	$7/8$ in diameter
Main jet:	160
Needle jet:	0.105
Pilot jet:	25
Slide:	375/3
Needle:	B

Wheels & tyres

Front:	3.25 x 17 in Dunlop Ribbed
Rear:	3.50 x 17 in Dunlop Universal

Brakes

Front:	7 in full-width hub – single leading shoe
Rear:	7 in drum – single leading shoe

Capacities (UK)

Petrol tank:	$3^{1}/2$ gal (16 l)
Oil tank:	5 pt (2.8 l)

Electrics

Generator:	Lucas RM13/15
Ignition:	Energy transfer
Battery:	Lucas PUZ7E-11

Colour All black – except the petrol tank in black top half, ivory lower half.

Dimensions

Wheelbase:	$51^{3}/4$ in (131.4 cm)
Ground clearance:	5 in (12.7 cm)
Width over handlebars:	26 in (66 cm)
Weight:	353 lb (160 kg)

1960 model: Unit construction T100A Tiger 100 model
Commencing Engine Number: H11512
Models: T100A Tiger 100
Associated 'C' range models: 350cc 3TA model Twenty-one
500 cc 5TA model Speed Twin

Engine
The 3TA and 5TA unit-construction aluminium alloy crankcase continued for 1960, but with the introduction of the E3325 sports-type camshafts E4022 and E4033 for the T100A model, which continued to utilise the original $3/4$ in radius cam followers (tappets) introduced on the Twenty One. No change was made to the one-piece forged steel crankshaft, or to the radial bolted-on central cast

Right side view of the 1960 T100A Tiger 100 model, introducing the over-square unit-construction engine, transmission and gearbox unit, with rear enclosure panelling

iron flywheel. The crankshaft assembly was pressure fed with lubricating oil on the right side via a $1^7/16$ in diameter (nominal) steel-backed copper lead-lined plain bearing bush, its deep central oil feed groove distributing the lubricant through matching feed holes in the crankshaft plain journal diameter.

Unlike its Tiger 100 predecessors, the T100A did not boast polished versions of the 5TA Speed Twin H section RR56 aluminium alloy connecting rods. Similarly, no change was made to the dry sump lubrication system utilising the familiar twin plunger oil pipe and the oil pressure relief valve and indicator. The aluminium alloy cylinder head originally introduced for the 500cc 5TA model was used without change for the T100A model, complete with cast iron valve guides and 5TA valves and springs, the major departure being the introduction of 9:1 compression ratio pistons within the commonised cast iron cylinder block, and steel capped aluminium alloy push rods to comply with the new sports camshaft requirements. The single carburettor alloy inlet manifold used for the 3TA and 5TA models was utilised for the T100A, and for this year alone the $7/8$ in choke Amal 375/35 Monobloc carburettor was standardised on both the 5TA and T100A models with a 160 main jet and an air filter.

The RM12 ac alternator specified for the 3TA and 5TA, with a rectifier to supply the combined six volt dc coil ignition and lighting circuits, gave way to the recently-introduced Lucas RM13/15 'Energy Transfer' ignition system. In this, a six pole magnetic rotor (in the case of the T100A) was peg located to the engine drive sprocket to ensure a 'timed' generator pulse created a maximum electrical energy pulse when the distributor contact breaker points opened to start the engine. The battery charging and lighting circuit were separate and independent from the ignition system.

Gearbox

The Triumph-designed four-speed standard road ratio gearbox used heavy duty shafts and gears of hardened nickel and nickel chrome steel, with a positive stop right-hand foot-operated change mechanism, incorporating an external gear position indicator. It had been continued without change from the previous 3TA and 5TA models.

The 20 tooth gearbox drive sprocket specified for the 5TA was also standardised on the T100A, together with the scroll-operated clutch thrust mechanism contained within the polished gearbox outer cover.

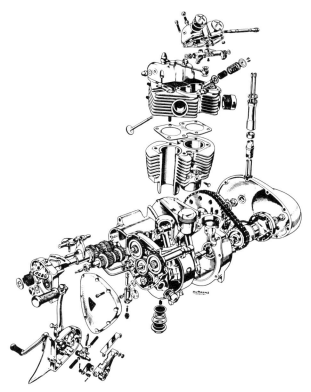

Exploded diagram of the unit-construction Tiger 100 engine and gearbox assembly

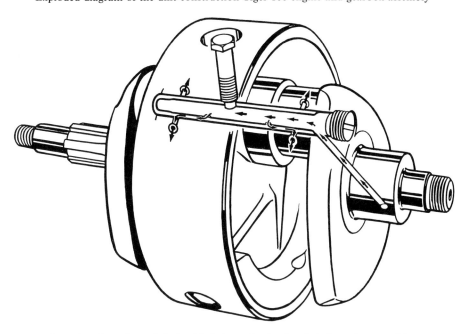

One-piece forged crankshaft with bolt-on flywheel and sludge tube assembly

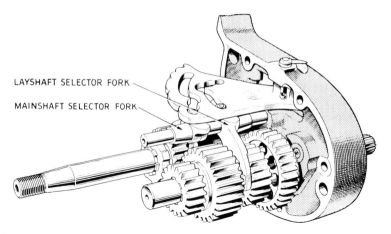

LAYSHAFT SELECTOR FORK

MAINSHAFT SELECTOR FORK

The compact inner cover assembly mounting the mainshaft, layshaft and selectors

Primary Transmission

A multi-plate clutch mounted on the end of the gearbox mainshaft and located within the oil-containing polished aluminium chaincase had its driving plates incorporating Langite friction lining element increased to five, with six driven plates. This necessitated increased dimensional changes to provide a deeper clutch sprocket and housing, clutch centre, longer springs and spring cups and also longer clutch operating rod. The clutch centre itself enclosed a four armed hub 'spider' located by four drive and four rebound shock absorbing rubbers. The primary drive was transmitted through a $3/8$ in pitch duplex chain via a 26 tooth engine sprocket and a 58 tooth clutch sprocket. A new fully-adjustable Neoprene-backed spring blade chain tensioner had been introduced also in the 5TA model for this year.

Frame

The entirely new 'lowered' lightweight brazed cradle frame had been introduced with the 3TA and 5TA models, incorporating an hydraulically-damped rear swinging arm. It had remained common to all the models in the range since its introduction in 1957. For this year the new T100A model specified the same Girling rear suspension units as those fitted to the 3TA Twenty One model, only the 'toothpaste' type Tiger 100 badge on the black-finished rear enclosure panels being different from that of the previous year's models. The rear frame now incorporated four brackets hidden behind the panelling, facilitating subsequent fitment of a luggage carrier and pannier equipment. An 'Easy-Lift' centre-stand was fitted, but no provision was made for fitment of an anti-theft steering lock.

Forks

The Triumph-type telescopic fork with internal two-way oil-controlled damping and incorporating a Triumph-patented integral headlamp and instrument nacelle was continued. It contained the internally illuminated, rubber-mounted speedometer and ammeter, and was identical to that of the 3TA and 5TA models, apart from a revised nacelle top cover to accommodate the Lucas 41SA lighting switch and SS5 ignition cut-out button used on the T100A model.

The manually-operated steering damper knob and stem was located to the rear of the nacelle.

Fuel Tank

An all-welded $3^{1}/_{2}$ (imp) gallon steel fuel tank with fore and aft mounting lugs formed by twin parallel straight struts passing right through the central tank shell provided the triangulated stiffening member between the frame head and seat lugs.

Triumph 'mouth organ' tank badges were fitted, in conjunction with moulded rubber kneepads. Chrome decorative trim was applied to the tank top seam and tank sides, from the front tunnel to the knee grips. A chrome tank top parcel grid and quick release petrol filler cap were fitted as standard equipment. A single cork-type fuel tap provided both main and reserve facility.

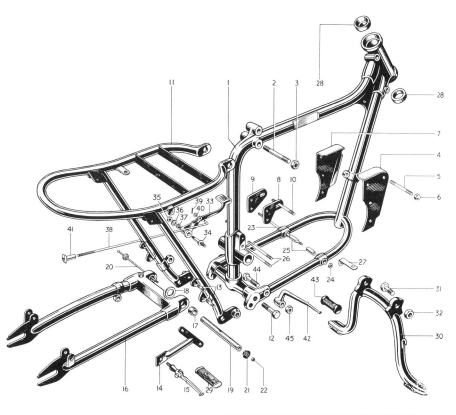

Index No.	Description.	Index No.	Description.
1	Frame, front.	24	Nut.
2	Stud, seat tube top.	25	Distance piece.
3	Nut.	26	Stud, engine plate to frame.
4	Plate front, R.H. engine.	27	Stay, exhaust pipe.
5	Stud, plate to frame.	28	Cup, steering head.
6	Nut, domed.	29	Rubber, pillion footrest.
7	Plate, front L.H. engine.	30	Stand, centre.
8	Plate, rear R.H. engine.	31	Bolt, stand.
9	Plate, rear L.H. engine.	32	Nut.
10	Stud, engine rear.	33	Pedal, brake.
11	Frame, rear.	34	Spindle, brake pedal.
12	Bolt, seat tube bottom.	35	Nut.
13	Stud, pillion footrest plate.	36	Washer.
14	Plate, pillion footrest.	37	Washer, spring.
15	Pillion footrest.	38	Rod, brake operating.
16	Fork, swinging.	39	Split pin, rod to pedal.
17	Bush, fork pivot.	40	Washer.
18	Washer, distance.	41	Nut, brake adjuster.
19	Spindle.	42	Footrest.
20	Rod, retaining.	43	Rubber, footrest.
21	Cap.	44	Bolt, footrest.
22	Nut.	45	Nut.
23	Stud, engine bottom.		

The T100A frame arrangement with swan-neck type headlug, and rear swinging arm   93

Oil Tank

A separate 5 (imp) pint 'bolt-on' oil tank was provided within the rear enclosure and fitted with a screw filler cap, vent pipe and extended oil tank filter unit. A branched 'twig' was incorporated in the return oil line to provide a light pressure positive feed to the rocker box spindles.

Brakes

Front: Full-width hub, heavily finned with 7 in diameter leading shoe drum brake.

Rear: 7 in diameter cast-iron drum with integral 43 tooth rear chain sprocket.

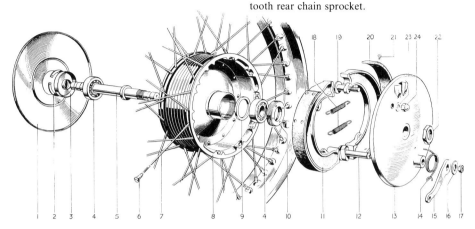

Index No.	Description.	Index No.	Description.
1	Plate, L.H. cover.	13	Plate, brake anchor.
2	Circlip, L.H. bearing.	14	Spring, lever return.
3	Cover, dust.	15	Lever, brake operating.
4	Bearing, ball journal.	16	Washer.
5	Spindle.	17	Nut, brake lever.
6	Nipple, spoke.	18	Spring, shoe return.
7	Spoke.	19	Pin, shoe fulcrum.
8	Hub and brake drum.	20	Lining, brake.
9	Ring, bearing backing.	21	Rivet, brake lining.
10	Ring nut, bearing.	22	Nut, plate to spindle.
11	Shoe c/w lining.	23	Washer.
12	Cam, brake operating.	24	Nut, fulcrum pin.

The seven inch diameter cast-iron full-width hub, housing the single leading shoe front brake assembly mounted on the aluminium alloy anchor plate

Wheels

Triumph design front and rear wheels with plated spokes were fitted to WM2-17 chrome-plated rims, front and rear.

Tyres

Dunlop 3.25 x 17 in Ribbed front, 3.50 x 17 in Universal rear.

Mudguards

A 'firemans helmet' type of deep valanced steel front mudguard carried the chrome, bevelled Triumph front number plate, as fitted to the contemporary Thunderbird model, but required an oft lost chromed wedge to accommodate the smaller radius 'C' range guard. The front mudguard stay acted as a front stand to facilitate front wheel removal.

The steel rear mudguard was mounted within the rear enclosure panels, and carried the rubber-mounted tool tray beneath the hinged twinseat. From engine number H13115 the rear enclosure panel rear jointing flange was changed to face outwards, considerably assisting assembly and subsequent dismantling procedures.

Exhaust System
The original $1^{1}/_{2}$ in diameter exhaust pipes used for the 3TA and 5TA models were now also used on the new T100A. The silencers specified, although outwardly similar with asymetric inlets and centre-stand accommodating 'dimples', incorporated glass wool packed straight-through exits, baffled only by the strangely fluted silencer mutes.

Air Filter
A metal-clad boxed air filter was frame-mounted in line with the carburettor inlet, immediately behind the rear enclosure panels.

Electrical Equipment
The Lucas RM13/15 energy transfer ac generator system comprised an alternator with separate ignition and lighting windings and a 6 pole rotating magnet rotor. The two stator ignition windings were connected direct to the inlet camshaft-driven Lucas 18D2 distributor, and in parallel with the energy transfer ignition coil, an over-riding earthing cut-out button being fitted into the nacelle instrument panel. The four lighting coils fed directly to the full-wave rectifier, an intermediate tapping feeding the Lucas 41SA lighting switch which controlled the charging rate according to the lighting demand. The direct current was passed to the Lucas 6 volt PUZE 12 amp hour battery via an ammeter. The battery fed the lighting section of the switch in the nacelle top cover which controlled the 7 in 30/24 watt pre-focus headlamp in the adjustable nacelle light unit and the Lucas L564 combined stop/tail lamp.

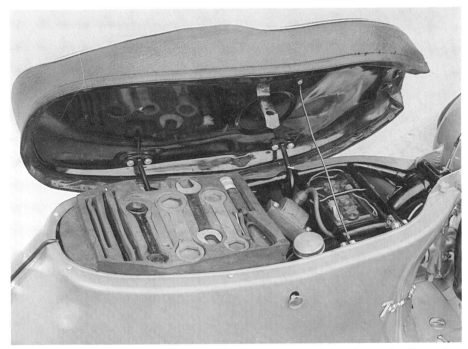

The hinged Twinseat, rear enclosure panelling and rubber moulded tool tray, also illustrating the battery and energy transfer ignition coil location and mounting

Speedometer
A Smiths 120 mph (180 kph) Chronometric speedometer instrument with internal illumination was fitted, with separate odometer and trip recorder, driven by a Smiths rear wheel drive gearbox.

Tachometer
Not fitted.

Handlebars
One inch diameter chrome-plated handlebars were fitted, with a Triumph quick-action twistgrip incorporating a knurled friction adjuster knob. The chrome brake and clutch levers, with chrome mounting brackets incorporating cable adjusters had a combined horn push and headlight dipswitch attached to the left-hand lever bracket.

Twinseat
A Triumph hinged Twinseat with latex foam cushion and covered in black waterproof 'Vynide' with a black top, white piping, black sides and a black rim trim band was specified. The seat catch incorporated a sprung plunger and a removable, screwed, chrome 'anti-thief' knob type of latch mechanism, the seat being restrained by a simple check strap. A passenger safety strap was available as an optional extra.

Finish
Frame	Black
Forks	Black
Mudguards – front	Black
– rear enclosure panels	Black
Fuel tank	Black top, ivory lower half
Oil tank	Black

Extras
Quickly detachable rear wheel (43 teeth)
Pillion footrests, prop stand
Twinseat safety strap

US Alternatives
US high rise handlebar
US throttle, brake and clutch cables to match above
Twinseat safety strap

The 1961 T100A 'Tiger 100' model. It was at engine number H22430 that the energy transfer ignition system was replaced by a normal battery/coil ignition system

1961 model: Unit construction T100A Tiger 100 model
Commencing Engine Number: H18612
Models: T100A Tiger 100 (with TR5A – UK general export and TR5AC and TR5AR competition variants for the US Market).
Associated 'C' range models: 500cc 5TA Speed Twin
                                     350 cc 3TA Twenty One

Left side view of one of the factory's own 1961 TR5AC competition models, with ET ignition and direct lighting

Left side view of the 1961 TR5AR, with ET ignition and battery lighting

Engine

The engine unit for the new 1961 TR5A models was virtually identical to that of the original 1960 T100A model, which itself continued for 1961, but with the inlet camshaft specification changed to E3134 form on all models and also introduced as the exhaust camshaft on the T100A and TR5A models.

No other changes in the 1960 specification were made, although the oil pressure relief valve now incorporated a new captive 'O' ring in the cap to obviate oil seepage, and the T100A model adopted full coil ignition from engine number H22430.

Gearbox

No change was made to the standard 'road' internal ratios for the T100A models. The TR5AC model, however, was fitted with wide ratio gears in the 'first condition' (See gear condition/ratio chart). This year the left-hand poro-phosphor bronze layshaft bush contained within the inner gearbox casing was changed on T100A and all TR5 variants to a caged needle roller bearing in association with a pegged phosphor bronze thrust washer, necessitating a revised layshaft journal diameter. The previous final drive gearbox sprocket was replaced by one of 19 teeth for the T100A and TR5AR models and 17 teeth in the case of the TR5AC variant. A folding kickstart continued to be fitted as standard equipment.

Primary Transmission

No change was made to the multi-plate clutch although improved non-stick Langite clutch material drive plates were now specified.

Frame

A new front frame section was used in 1961, permitting adjustment to the fork steering lockstops, and made common on all models in the range. A new rear frame section was introduced on the new TR5A models, providing a mounting for the new Lucas MLZ9E battery and associate carrier, tool carrier and revised oil tank with quick release filler cap and anti-froth tower. The T100A continued with the full rear enclosure panels whilst on TR5A models a full conventional 'Sports' rear mudguard was specified together with integral, dual-purpose rear stays and a lifting handle. The 'Easy-Lift' centre stand continued, with a 'taller' version for the TR5AC and AR models which had larger diameter wheels and tyres. No provision was made for an anti-theft steering lock.

Forks

The Triumph telescopic fork continued for 1961, now incorporating aluminium spacer sleeves in lieu of the previous rolled steel type. On T100A models the nacelle top changed at H22430 to accomodate a Lucas PRS8 switch as a result of the changeover from energy transfer to full 6 volt coil ignition. A conventional gaitered fork with headlamp-mounting top fork covers was introduced for the TR5A models.

Fuel Tank

In the case of the competition TR5A and TR5AC models, a new $2^1/2$ (Imp) gallon saddle tank was specified in conjunction with an additional frame stiffening strut, a direct result of US experience with the earlier T100A models converted locally to competition trim. It was fitted with quick-release filler cap and jack chain and twin lever PTFE-treated internal taper fuel taps.

The T100A fuel tank continued as per the 1960 model.

Oil Tank

As 1960 model.

Brakes

This year both front and rear brake shoes were made fully floating, providing a 25% improvement in overall braking efficiency. Otherwise specification as 1960 model.

Wheels

The T100A specification remained unchanged. The TR5AC model was equipped with a 3.25 x 19 in Trials Universal at the front and a 400 x 18 in Trials Universal at the rear, whereas the TR5AR model had a Dunlop Universal 3.25 x 19 in ribbed front tyre and a Dunlop Universal 3.50 x 18 in rear.

The saddle-type fuel tank fitted to the TR5AC competition models. The frame stiffening strut was bolted to the original tank mounting points, and a lower steady mounted on the main frame top rail. Later model tank straps were turnbuckle restrained, and fabricated in stainless steel

Mudguards

The new TR5A sports model variants now specified a plain steel front mudguard whereas the T100A continued with the 'firemans helmet' type. Both utilised the front stay as a front wheel stand, when required. The Sports machine also specified a conventional rear mudguard, its rear stays functioning as lifting handles. The T100A continued with an internal rear mudguard and full rear enclosure panelling.

Exhaust System

The 1961 T100A and the TR5AR models continued with twin downswept exhaust pipes and silencers whereas the TR5AC model was fitted with a 2 into 1 upswept exhaust pipe and a single right-hand silencer.

Air Filter

The TR5A models now specified a detachable chrome pancake-type air filter with a replaceable paper-type element, mounted on the single carburettor. The T100A air filter remained located behind the rear enclosure panelling, and was modified later in the season to become an interchangeable unit with a replaceable element.

Electrical equipment

The T100A, TR5AC and AR models commenced the 1961 season with Lucas RM13/15 energy transfer ignition and a separate 6 volt dc battery charging and lighting system. At engine number H21122 in the case of the TR5A and TR5AR models, and at engine number H22430 on the T100A models, the electrical system was converted to the Lucas 6V battery coil ignition system currently in   99

1961 models introduced fully floating brake shoes providing improved 'bite' and braking performance

use on the 3TA and 5TA models. The TR5AC competition model retained the energy transfer ignition system up to 1962.

1961 Energy Transfer System (with distributor)

The alternator ignition section (2 stator coils) was connected directly to the distributor, 2ET ignition coil and cut-out button circuit at a single junction. The ac pulses were triggered by the inlet camshaft-operated Lucas 18D2 distributor which now operated over a 10° auto-advance range on the T100A and TR5AR, and on the battery-less TR5AC models (stator 47177 with or without lights) with a 5° auto-advance range.

On road machines fitted with a battery (stator 47149), the lighting coils fed via a full-wave rectifier to the 12AH 6 volt battery through an ammeter in the headlamp. The Lucas 41SA switch in the nacelle top cover (T100A) selected the alternator output to match the lighting load presented by the 30/24 watt pre-focus headlight bulb in the 7 in headlamp and the 6/18 watt stop/tail light bulb in the Lucas L564 rear lamp unit.

Coil Ignition System (with distributor)

Finally introduced on the T100A model at engine number H22430, the 6 volt coil ignition system comprised a Lucas RM13/15 alternator feeding alternating current to a full-wave bridge rectifier connected to the battery via the ammeter. The battery fed the PRS8 lighting switch, which incorporated an additional switching circuit connected to the alternator windings, thereby selecting the appropriate charging current to suit the lighting load.

An 'emergency start' ignition switching position fed direct alternator pulses to provide limited start and run conditions in the event of a flat battery, the normal ignition 'On' position feeding the single ignition coil which was triggered by a 15° auto advance range unit within the Lucas 18D2 distributor.

Speedometer

A fork top lug mounting bracket on TR5AR and TR5AC models accommodated the speedometer, which remained nacelle-mounted on the T100A models.

Tachometer

Not fitted.

Handlebars

1 in diameter handlebars continued to be fitted to the T100A model, whereas $^7/8$ in diameter sports-type flat handlebars were fitted to the new TR5A variants, incorporating brake and clutch controls with ball-ended levers on US market models. The Triumph adjustable friction twistgrip continued on the T100A model, whilst an Amal twistgrip was now used on the $^7/8$ in diameter handlebars. A combined horn push and dipswitch was fitted to the clutch lever bracket on both models, all control lever brackets featuring cable adjusters.

Twinseat

The finish at the commencement of the season was as previously, but was changed mid-season to grey top, white piping, black sides and grey rim trim band for the US market models.

Finish	T100A	TR5A
Frame	Black	Black
Forks	Black/silver sheen	Black
Mudguards – front	Silver sheen	Silver sheen with kingfisher blue central stripe/ gold lined
– rear	n/a	Silver sheen with kingfisher blue central stripe/ gold lined
Rear enclosure panels	Silver sheen	n/a
Fuel tank	Black/silver sheen	Kingfisher blue/ silver sheen
Oil tank	Black	Black
Switch panel	n/a	Black

Extras

Quickly detachable rear wheel (43 tooth).
Pillion footrests.
Prop stand.
Twinseat safety strap.

US Alternatives

US high rise handlebars.
US brake, throttle and clutch cables to suit above.
Ball-ended clutch and front brake levers.
Twinseat safety strap.

1962 model: Unit-construction T100SS Tiger 100 model
Commencing Engine Number: H25252
Models: T100SS, Tiger 100 with TR5A UK and general export models and TR5AR and T100SC competiton models for the US market.
Associated 'C' range models:-   5TA Speed Twin
3TA Twenty One

Engine

The basic engine unit for the T100S, TR5AR and new T100SC models continued almost unchanged from the previous year. However, the E4039 exhaust camshaft with E3134 racing form was   101

The 1962 version of the Tiger 100, now designated the T100SS, was equipped with 'bikini' side panels, and finally dispensed with the nacelle. It sported a right hand two-into-one downswept exhaust system with Resonator silencer

re-introduced on the new T100SC model, whereas the T100SS and US TR5AR continued with the softer E3325 sports exhaust cam form.

Gearbox
All models this year specified the standard road ratio Triumph four-speed gearbox.

Primary Transmission
As 1961 models.

Frame
'Bikini' style smaller rear enclosure panels were introduced on the T100SS model, and the 500cc competition models were now equipped with a conventional rear mudguard, Lucas MLZ9E battery,

The demand became sufficient to provide a four point system of attachment for a sidecar to the 'Tiger 100'

tool carrier and oil tank incorporating the quick release filler and anti-froth tower. No change was made to the rear swinging arm which accommodated a 4 in section rear tyre on the T100SC and TR5AR models, requiring lengthened suspension units (12.9 in in lieu of 11.9 in), alternative rate springing (100 lb/in in lieu of 130 lb/in), and associated lengthened centre and prop stands.

Forks
The Triumph telescopic pattern gaitered front fork with two-way damping continued for 1962, the nacelle being discontinued with the demise of the T100A model in favour of the large chromed headlamp (SS700P) on the T100SS, and the smaller black Lucas MCH 66 unit on the T100SC.

Fuel Tank
A $3^{1}/_{2}$ (imp) gallon steel fuel tank was specified for the T100SS model, whilst the TR5AR and T100SC were fitted with a 3.3 (US) gallon tank in conjunction with an additional frame stiffening strut. Both tank variants were equipped with quick release filler caps, those on the US competition models having a retaining jack chain. Separate main and reserve lever-type taps were used on the SC and AR competition models.

Oil Tank
As 1960 model but now incorporating quick release filler cap and anti-froth tower.

Brakes
As 1961 models.

Wheels
As 1961 Sports models.

Tyres
The new T100SS specified Dunlop 3.25 x 18 in Ribbed front and a 3.50 x 18 in Universal rear. TR5AC and TR5AR as 1961.

Mudguards
Plain painted steel sports guards, front and rear, the front guard rear stays also functioning as a front wheel stand and the rear guard stays acting as rear lifting handles. 1962 marked the end of the chrome plated bezelled front number plate.

Exhaust System
All the T100 models and variants this year specified right-hand downswept 2 into 1 exhaust pipes with a single silencer. The T100SC model utilised the bigger straight-through 'Resonator' sports silencer.

Air Filter
For this year, all the T100 variants were fitted with a pancake-type air filter, incorporating a replaceable felt element, the US competition models specifying an additional chrome water deflector.

Electrical Equipment
The newly-introduced Lucas RM19 alternator equipment for 1962 provided 6 volt coil ignition on the T100SS and TR5AR models, the energy transfer system being retained for the T100SC model.

Energy transfer system T100SC model (with distributor)
The new RM19 energy transfer system was designed to provide battery-less lighting with independent direct ignition, the four lead (47173) stator providing ignition via a contact breaker/distributor to both spark plugs. The lighting system was removable for competition events. The distributor (40820) range was reduced to 5 degrees (10° engine) to improve spark performance, and gave an excellent full advanced ignition characteristic with adequate starting spark energy. A separate 'kill' button was fitted to the right-hand handlebar to stop the engine.

Coil ignition system – T100SS, TR5A and TR5AR models

The new RM19 ac generator was fitted, feeding the battery with dc via a full wave rectifier and ammeter, the output controlled by a Lucas PRS8 switch in the LG 'Bikini' rear enclosure panel. The ignition section of this switch also provided an additional 'EMG' emergency start facility in the event of a flat battery, its normal function being to supply battery current to the ignition coil which was triggered via the contact breaker within the distributor assembly.

Lighting was provided by a 6 volt 30/24 watt adjustable pre-focus headlamp, with a parking bulb at the front and a combined Lucas stop/tail lamp at the rear.

Speedometer
Fork top bracket mounting Smiths Chronometric 120 mph (180 kph), with internal illumination, separate odometer and trip recorder with re-set.

Tachometer
Not fitted.

Handlebars
7/8 diameter handlebars were now standardised on all models, which used an Amal adjustable friction twistgrip. An engine cutout button was now fitted on the left for energy transfer ignition-equipped models, otherwise the specification followed that for the 1961 models. Ball-ended control levers were used on all competition models.

Twinseat
The Triumph designed hinged Twinseat continued for 1962, now with grey top for all markets, the US version (West Coast) having a passenger safety strap fitted to comply with state laws.

Finish	T100SS	T100SC	TR5A	TR5AR
Frame	Black	Black	Black	Black
Forks	Black	Black	Black	Black
Mudguards – front	Silver sheen with kingfisher blue central stripe, lined gold	Silver sheen with burgundy central stripe, lined gold	Silver sheen with kingfisher blue central stripe, lined gold	Silver sheen with burgundy central stripe, lined gold
– rear	Silver sheen with kingfisher blue central stripe, lined gold	Silver sheen with burgundy central stripe, lined gold	Silver sheen with kingfisher blue central stripe, lined gold	Silver sheen with burgundy central stripe, lined gold
Rear enclosure panels	Kingfisher blue	–	–	–
*Fuel tank	Kingfisher blue and silver sheen, lined gold	Burgundy and silver sheen, lined gold	Kingfisher blue and silver sheen	Burgundy and silver sheen, lined gold
Oil tank	Black	Black	Black	Black

*Top half of colour of tank shown first.

Extras
Quickly detachable rear wheel (43T)
Pillion footrests
Propstand
Twinseat safety strap

US alternatives
US high rise bars
US brake, throttle and clutch cables for above
Ball-ended clutch and front brake levers
Twinseat safety strap

Right side view of the 1963 T100SS, now equipped with exhaust camshaft-driven twin 4CA contact breakers, and twin ignition coils mounted beneath the fuel tank. The two-into-one right hand exhaust system sported a beefed looking Resonator silencer. The bikini side panels had now been styled to provide a sleeker appearance

1963 model: Unit-construction T100SS Tiger 100 model
Commencing Engine Number: H29733
Models: T100SS, Tiger 100 with T100SR (Road) and SC (Competition) variants for the US market.
Associated 'C' range models: 5TA Speed Twin
                                                      T90 Tiger 90
                                                      3TA Twenty-one

Engine

The inlet camshafts on all three Tiger 100 variants were now fitted with the E3134 racing cam form, all three now specifying exhaust camshafts of the E3325 sports type. These inlet and exhaust cams were used in conjunction with $3/4$ in radius cam followers (tappets). A new timing chest cover incorporated a Lucas 4CA twin contact breaker assembly and auto advance mechanism, driven from the right-hand end of the exhaust camshaft. The associated inlet camshaft no longer carried the distributor spiral gear drive. The steel-capped alloy push rods operated the overhead valve train in a new aluminium alloy cylinder head of greater overall depth, thus allowing a thinner and more flexible copper cylinder head gasket (E4675 replacing E4015). The rocker box caps had serrated edges to match the (Amal) locking 'click' springs, fitted to prevent subsequent loosening in service. The cast iron cylinder barrel remained unchanged, but internally the aluminium alloy RR56 connecting rods were now polished and fitted with Vandervell VP3 big end bearing liners. The crankcase now incorporated provision for a tachometer drive take-off point at the left-hand end of the exhaust camshaft, in conjunction with an associated 'press-in' drive thimble.

Gearbox

The Triumph four-speed gearbox now featured a closer second gear pair (known at the factory as the 'mangle gears' due to their stubby and robust appearance!) The gear change camplate this year incorporated a bridge piece to strengthen the outer track, to prevent it 'opening-up' under heavy use in competition. In other respects the gearbox specification remained unchanged.

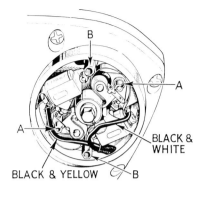

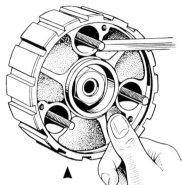

B

A

A

BLACK & WHITE

BLACK & YELLOW   B

The 3 vane clutch shock absorber unit employed on the 1963 model range

Primary Transmission

The multi-plate clutch had a redesigned three vane shock absorber mounted in the clutch centre, to replace the earlier four vane version. This called for new clutch pins, springs, cups and pressure plate. No other changes were made.

Frame

New front and rear frame sections appeared for 1963, the front revised to accommodate twin ignition coils mounted under the fuel tank. The rear section was redesigned to accept a new rubber-mounted oil tank, and mounting brackets for the alternative vertical location of the 'under the tank' tyre inflator. The T100SS, SR and SC models now incorporated much more stylish 'Bikini' rear enclosure panels, the left-hand side carrying the Lucas 88SA separate ignition and lighting switches. Conventional rear mudguards were fitted. The Lucas MLZ9E 6 volt battery (where fitted) was now housed in a new style carrier, with a new tool tray and oil tank, all rubber-mounted within the rear frame. The oil tank featured a quick release filler cap and an anti-froth tower. The rear swinging arm continued unchanged to accommodate the 4 inch section rear tyre specified for the competition SC versions for which neither battery nor battery carrier were specified. All models featured the Triumph 'Easy-Lift' centre stand.

Forks

The 650cc (black/green) internal fork springs were standardised this year for all three models. The fork top brackets accommodated a large chrome headlamp on the T100SS and SR models, the 'battery-less' energy transfer T100SC model having a small black Lucas MCH 66 headlamp unit.

Fuel Tank

A new 3 (imp) gallon fuel tank was fitted to both the T100SS and East Coast US T100SR road models, the West Coast SR and SC models having a new $2^{1}/_{2}$ US gallon fuel tank mounted on a frame/tank strut. Both tanks had underside recesses to accommodate the relocated twin ignition coils, and were fitted with chrome quick release filler caps, the US versions having in addition a cap-retaining jack chain. In all other respects the specification remained that of the 1962 models.

Oil Tank

A new 5 (imp) pint rubber-mounted oil tank with separate drain plug was now fitted, a crimping in the return line at the filler neck providing the necessary restriction to create oil pressure in the rocker feed pipe branch.

Brakes

As 1961 models, but now with 46 tooth rear wheel integral brake drum and sprocket on standard and quickly detachable rear wheels.

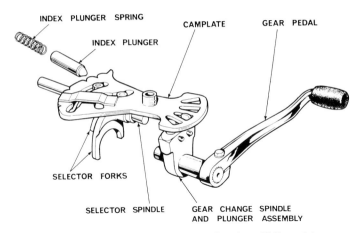

INDEX PLUNGER SPRING

INDEX PLUNGER

CAMPLATE

GEAR PEDAL

SELECTOR FORKS

SELECTOR SPINDLE

GEAR CHANGE SPINDLE
AND PLUNGER ASSEMBLY

Bridged gearchange camplate introduced on 1963 models

Wheels

A WM2 x 18 front wheel rim was specified for the T100SS model, and a WM 2 x 19 for the T100SR and SC models. Rear wheel rims were WM2 x 18 for the T100SS and US East Coast SR models and WM3 x 18 for the US West Coast SR and both SC models.

Tyres

Dunlop 3.25 x 18 Ribbed front and 3.50 x 18 Universal rear on UK models, with Dunlop 3.25 x 19 Ribbed front and Dunlop 3.50 x 18 (SR) or 4.00 x 18 Universal rear on US models.

Mudguards

This was the last year in which the US models carried the 'pedestrian slicer' front number plate.

Exhaust System

The 1963 season continued with the right side 2 into 1 downswept system and its associated 'Resonator' silencer for the T100SS model and US road-going SR models. A left-hand 2 into 1 upswept pipe and small sports silencer was fitted to the two US SC models.

Sectional details of the 1963 Resonator silencer

Air filter

The chrome pancake-type air filter unit with unpierced upper section to deflect water drops and replaceable felt element was now specified for all models.

Electrical equipment

1963 saw the deletion of the inlet camshaft-operated 18D2 distributor unit and single ignition coil in favour of the new-type exhaust camshaft-driven Lucas twin contact breaker and condenser assembly mounted within the engine timing cover and introducing twin ignition coils now mounted on the frame top rail beneath the fuel tank.

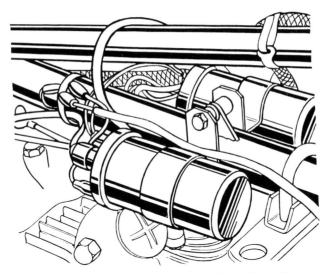

Twin ignition coil mounting beneath the fuel tank

Coil ignition models (twin contact breaker)

Now fitted with the new Lucas 4CA twin contact breaker system controlling twin Lucas MA6 6 volt ignition coils, but still using the earlier high output Lucas 47164 coil ignition stator, ML9E volt battery and SS700P pre-focus chrome headlamp, with 6 volt 30/24 watt headlamps bulb and 3 watt pilot. The lighting and ignition switches (now Type 88SA) were fitted in the left panel.

Energy transfer system – (twin contact breaker)

The T100SC models for both US coasts specified the new Lucas RM19 five lead stator for twin contact breaker operation. Ignition was direct from the alternator coils to the twin 3ET ignition coils and condensers, mounted on the frame beneath the fuel tank and linked electrically to the twin contact breakers. The handlebar-mounted Lucas S5 cut-out button shorted together both ignition coil feeds, neutralising the contact breakers. The lighting system required no battery, ammeter or rectifier, feeding the lights directly with ac current according to switching demand. The detachable MCH66 adjustable headlamp was fitted with a 6 volt 24/24 watt head/dip pre-focus bulb. The dip and lighting switch was installed in the headlamp, and the horn and ignition cut-out switches were handlebar-mounted, with a Lucas L564 (6/18 watt) stop/tail lamp at the rear.

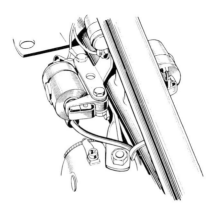

108   Twin energy transfer coils mounted beneath the fuel tank

Speedometer
As 1962 models.

Tachometer
Not fitted.

Handlebars
The previous year's $^7/_8$ inch diameter 'flat sports' type handlebars continued to be fitted to all T100 variants. The competition models continued to feature ball-ended clutch and front brake levers.

Twinseat
As 1960 models, but now with rubber bump stop on to the top frame rail. The new part number was dropped later in the season.

Finish	T100SS	T100SR	T100SC
Frame	Black	Black	Black
Forks	Black	Black	Black
Mudguards – front	Silver	Silver	Silver
– rear	Silver	Silver	Silver
Rear enclosure panels	Silver	Silver	Silver
*Fuel tank	Regal purple and silver	Regal purple and silver	Regal purple and silver
Oil tank	Black	Black	Black
Switch panel	Black	Black	–

*Top half colour of tank shown first.

Extras
Quickly detachable rear wheel (46T)
Pillion footrests
Propstand
Twinseat safety strap

US alternatives
US high rise handlebars
US brake throttle and clutch cables for above
Ball-ended clutch and front brake levers
Twinseat safety strap

1964 model: Unit-construction T100SS Tiger 100 model
Commencing Engine Number: H32465
Model: T100SS Tiger 100 with T100 SR (Road) and SC (Competition) variants for the US market
Associated 'C' range models: 5TA Speed Twin
T90 Tiger 90
3TA Twenty One

Engine
The engine continued virtually unaltered for 1964. The push rod cover tube lower seals were now retained within new bottom cups, to ensure positive retention. A reinforced 'press-in' slotted tachometer drive thimble was substituted, to overcome a year of cable drive failures. These constituted the only changes in specification to the engine.

Right side view of the 1964 T100SS Tiger 100 model, the front forks now having external springs and heavy duty oil seals. The Bikini side panels had now been discontinued.

Gearbox

The Triumph four-speed gearbox was now fitted with needle roller bearings to support the layshaft at both ends, the second additional needle roller bearing replacing the floating bronze bush within the kickstart spindle. The T100SS, T100SR and US West Coast competition models adopted entirely new tooth form strengthened standard ratio-gear sets, the competition models for the US East Coast also specifying a new tooth form 'third condition' wide-ratio gear set. The clutch operation changed from the easily worn diecast scroll thrust mechanism to that of a more durable pressed steel three-ball operation, allowing clutch cable replacement without need to remove the outer cover, a feature that continued until the model ended in 1973.

Primary Transmission

The multi-plate clutch continued unchanged from 1963, the sole variation being the introduction on the US models of Armstrong cork linings, a material shipped from the States by the distributors for use on their own machines.

Frame

The 1963 front frame continued into 1964. The rear frame carrying the rubber-mounted oil tank and battery box had slight machining modifications to the pillion footrest and silencer bracket mounting lugs, to accommodate the new flat triangular mounting plates introduced with the twin downswept exhaust pipe and silencer systems. All variants of the T100 now had the rear enclosure styling panels discontinued, the ignition/lighting switches being accommodated within a new left-hand switch panel. Conventional sports-type rear mudguards were fitted, a new reinforced steel type for road models, and for the first time on a production model, Triumph polished aluminium alloy mudguards on the US competition models. The rear swinging arm continued unchanged, a crankcase undershield (skid plate) being specified for US competition models. The Triumph 'Easy Lift' centre stand was specified for all road models.

R/H side view of the the US version of the 1964 T100SR, Speed Tiger

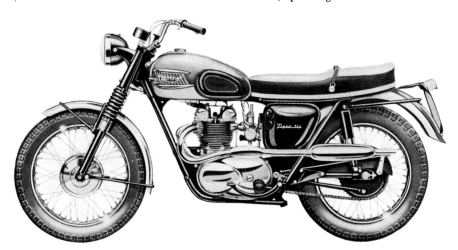

Left side view of the US version of the T100SC Sports Tiger

Forks
Triumph telescopic forks with larger fork oil seals and external springs with rubber gaiters were specified for all T100 variants. The shorter fork top brackets accommodated a large chrome headlamp on the T100SS and SR models, whilst the battery-less energy transfer T100SC model continued with the smaller competition headlamp unit. The manually-operated steering damper now incorporated an 'unwind' and anti-rattle rubber sleeve.

Fuel Tank
As 1963 models.

111

The improved push rod cover tube sealing arrangements introduced in 1964

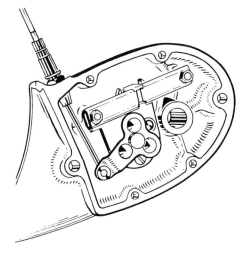

Illustrating the three ball clutch operating thrust mechanism used on 1964 models

The 1964 external spring front fork assembly

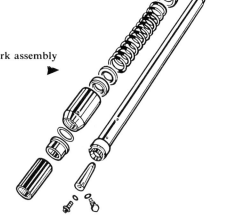

Sports front guard and fixings

Oil Tank
As 1963 models.

Brakes
As 1963 models.

Wheels
The front and rear wheels continued unchanged from the previous year.

Tyres
Dunlop 3.25 x 18 K70 Ribbed front and 3.50 x 18 K70 Gold Seal Universal rear on UK models, with Dunlop 3.25 x 19 K70 Universal front and 4.00 x 18 K70 Gold Seal Universal rear on US T100SR, and on T100SC Dunlop 3.50 x 19 K70 Gold Seal Universal front, with 4.00 x 18 K70 Gold Seal Universal (West Coast) or 4.00 x 18 Trials Universal or Sports knobbly rear (East Coast).

Mudguards
Painted steel mudguards, of improved reinforced 'Trophy' pattern were fitted this year for both front and rear of the T100SS and US SR road models. Other models continued unchanged.

Exhaust system
For 1964, the road-going T100SS and SR models were specified with twin downswept exhaust pipes, the T100SS having internally-baffled silencers. The US T100SR was specified with chrome plated straight through silencers. The US competition T100SC models continued to fit the left-hand 2-into-1 upswept enduro-type pipe and single silencer.

Air filter
The chrome pancake-type air filter continued to be fitted to all T100 models, with a replaceable element (felt for UK and General Export, paper for US models).

Electrical equipment
As 1963 models, US TR100R models now fitting the lower output RM19 47162 stator.

Speedometer and Tachometer
A new Smiths 'Anti-Vibration' magnetic speedometer was specified, in conjunction with matching tachometer, requiring an entirely new Metalastic bush mount on the T100SR front fork top lug. The speedometer was driven by a Smiths rear wheel-mounted speedometer drive gearbox, the tachometer being driven from the crankcase drive adaptor as previously. A tachometer was not fitted as standard on the T100SS and T100SC models.

1964 version Smiths magnetic speedometer and matching 'AV' tachometer used on US competition models, fitted to a Metalastic bush mounting on the fork top lug

Handlebars
As 1962 models.

Twinseat
As 1960 models.

Finish	T100SS	T100SR	T100SC
Frame	Black	Black	Black
Forks	Black	Black	Black
Mudguards – front	Silver with Hi-Fi scarlet stripe, lined gold	Silver with Hi-Fi scarlet stripe, lined gold	Polished alloy
– rear	Silver with Hi-Fi, scarlet stripe, lined gold	Silver with Hi-Fi scarlet stripe, lined gold	Polished alloy
*Fuel tank	Hi-Fi scarlet Hi-Fi scarlet and silver, lined in gold	Hi-Fi scarlet Hi-Fi scarlet and silver, lined in gold	Hi-Fi scarlet Hi-Fi scarlet and silver, lined in gold
Oil tank	Black	Black	Black
Switch panel	Black	Black	

*Top half colour of tank shown first.

Extras
Quickly detachable rear wheel (46T)
Pillion footrests
Propstand
Twinseat safety strap
Tachometer (T100SS).

US Alternatives
US high rise handlebars
US brake, throttle and clutch cables
Ball ended clutch and front brake levers
Twinseat safety strap
Crankcase sump plate

Left side view of the 1965 T100SS Tiger 100

1965 model: Unit-construction T100SS Tiger 100 model
Commencing Engine Number: H35987
Model: T100SS Tiger 100 with T100 SR (Road) and SC (Competition) variants
for the US market
Associated 'C' range models: 5TA Speed Twin
                                         T90 Tiger 90
                                         3TA Twenty-one

Engine
In a final attempt to cure oil leaks at the oil pressure relief valve the pressure indicator button and stem were deleted in favour of a blind domed cap. The original one-piece forged steel crankshaft with bolt-on flywheel assembly incorporating plain oil feed journals continued, but the flywheel now introduced a milled slot, designed to locate the crankshaft at top dead centre for ignition setting purposes. A threaded location hole was now incorporated into the crankcase left half, through which a special tool could be inserted. The reinforced press-in slotted tachometer drive thimble was continued, even though it had proved highly unsatisfactory and wear-prone in service.

The oil pressure relief valve with blind domed cap introduced on 1965 models

Gearbox
As 1964 models.

Primary Transmission
The only variation in the make-up of the 1965 clutch assembly from the previous year's version was the deletion of the expensive to import Armstrong cork clutch-facing material in favour of the new 'Neo-Langite' now fitted to all T100 variants.

Frame
As 1964 models.

Forks
The front forks were amended for 1965 to provide one inch of increased travel, with increased length stanchions, bottom outer members and inner damping sleeves. Longer, softer external fork springs were also fitted, together with a neater type of rubber gaiter and fork top covers.

Fuel Tank
A new increased capacity $3^{1}/_{2}$ (imp) gallon fuel tank was introduced, which no longer bolted to the frame head and seat lugs, to provide the integral frame stiffening member. This new tank was mounted directly on to the competition frame stiffening strut, in similar manner to the small competition tank introduced in 1962 to finally eliminate tank leakage problems on this model. The West Coast T100SR and both US Coast T100SC models continued with the previous small $2^{1}/_{2}$ (US) gallon competition tank and frame stiffening strut.

Oil Tank
The 1963 rubber-mounted oil tank continued unchanged.

Brakes
As 1963 models, except that the front brake anchor plate now incorporated an adjustable front   115

fulcrum pin and front cable abutment, replacing the previous abutment incorporated in the front sliding member. The rear brake anchor plate spindle bore was increased in diameter to allow rear brake shoe full area contact.

Wheels
The front and rear wheels continued for 1965 unchanged in almost every respect apart from a change in the front brake spindle to suit the new front forks. The brake shoe fulcrum pin was redesigned to provide full centering adjustment and extended to mount the front brake cable abutment. The quickly detachable rear wheel this year changed from taper roller bearings to plain journal bearings.

Tyres

UK and General Export		
	Front	Dunlop 3.25 x 18 K70 Ribbed
	Rear	Dunlop 3.50 x 18 K70 Gold Seal Universal
USA	T100SR & T100SC	
	Front	Dunlop 3.25 x 19 K70 Gold Seal Universal
	Rear	Dunlop 4.00 x 18 K70 Gold Seal Universal
	T100SC (East)	
	Front	Dunlop 3.50 x 19 Trials Universal or Sports Knobbly
	Rear	Dunlop 4.00 x 18 Trials Universal or Sports Knobbly

Mudguards
The front sports mudguards now utilised a tubular external central mounting bracket in place of the previous flat bridge. Otherwise as 1964 models.

Exhaust System
As 1964 models.

Air Filter
As 1964 models, the separate 'clip on' water deflector being discontinued in favour of a revised outer band with unpierced top section.

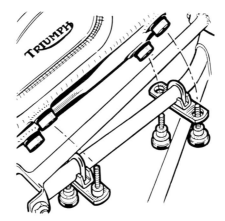

Illustration indicating the tank mounting method introduced on 1965 models

Electrical Equipment
Since the introduction of the Lucas 4CA twin contact breaker and auto advance mechanism in 1963, the only change made in 1965 was the standardisation of the medium output coil ignition stator (Lucas 47162) used on the US T100SR model for the T100SS model.

Speedometer and Tachometer
As 1964 models.

Handlebars
A slightly more rear-set $^7/_8$ in diameter 'flat sports' type of handlebar was fitted to the T100SS model,

the US T100SR now having the 'high-rise' equivalent, whereas the US T100SC model continued with the previous 'Enduro' type handlebar.

Twinseat
No change in specification was made for 1965, except that on East Coast T100SR and T100SC models seats with black tops and rim trim bands were specified.

Finish	T100SS	T100SR	T100SC
Frame	Black	Black	Black
Forks	Black	Black	Black
Mudguards – front	Alaskan white with Burnished gold stripe, lined gold	Alaskan white with Burnished gold stripe, lined gold	Alaskan white with Burnished gold stripe, lined gold
– rear	Alaskan white with Burnished gold stripe, lined gold	Alaskan white with Burnished gold stripe, lined gold	Alaskan white with Burnished gold stripe, lined gold
*Fuel tank	Burnished gold and Alaskan white lined gold	Burnished gold and Alaskan white lined gold	Burnished gold and Alaskan white lined gold
Oil tank	Black	Black	Black
Switch panel	Black	Black	

*Top half colour of tank shown first.

Extras
Quickly detachable rear wheel (46T)
Pillion footrests
Propstand
Twinseat safety strap
Tachometer (T100SS model).

US alternatives
US high rise handlebars
US brake, throttle and clutch cables for above
Ball-ended clutch and front brake levers
Twinseat safety strap
Crankcase sump plate

Left side view of the 1966 Tiger 100 model. Visual changes were the 'winged emblem' tank badges, stick-on kneegrips and Yale-type ignition switch

117

Left side view of East Coast US T100C competition model, equipped with left hand upswept exhaust system and folding footpegs

1966 model: Unit-construction T100 Tiger 100 model
Commencing Engine Number: H40528
Model: T100 Model Tiger 100 with T100R (Road) and T100C (Competition) variants for the US market
Associated 'C' range models: 5TA Speed Twin
                                 T90 Tiger 90
                                 3TA Twenty One

Engine
The engine continued unchanged apart from the use of a new induction heat-treated intermediate wheel, complete with bronze bush, from which the pinion teeth had been cut and subsequently heat-treated. The alloy cylinder head now specified Hidural inlet and exhaust valve guides and increased valve loading inner valve springs were fitted.

Gearbox
A crankcase protector to guide a broken rear chain safely round the gearbox sprocket was introduced for the first time. This was the only change in specification for 1966.

Primary Transmission
No changes were made for the 1966 season except for the introduction of a more durable chain tensioner blade.

Frame
The Tiger 100 front and rear frame sections were amended for 1966, the front section now incorporating the integral frame stiffening strut. The rear section brackets were modified to accept the rubber-mounted 12 volt battery equipment and increased capacity (6 imp pint) oil tank. The rear swinging arm was now capable of accepting sports 'Knobbly' tyres. On coil ignition models a left switch panel was fitted, incorporating both ignition (Yale-type key and lock barrel) and lighting switches, whereas the T100C without battery and rectifier had no switch panel fitted. Reinforced conventional steel rear mudguards were fitted to the road-going T100, T100R models and East Coast T100C models, the West Coast competition model continuing with polished aluminium mudguards. An improved tool tray was bolted to the rear mudguard, beneath the hinged twinseat.

Left side view of the West Coast US T100C, specified with polished alloy 'fenders'

Forks

The previous year's front forks continued for 1966. The US East Coast T100C assembly now incorporated a new internal piston and rod-type damper, together with heavy duty competition-type fork springs.

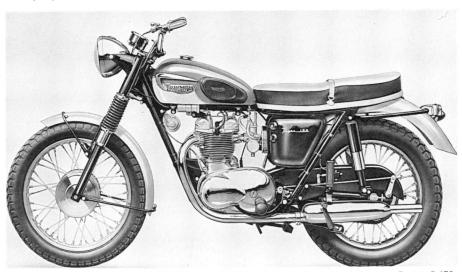

Left side view of the 1966 US T100R model. Note the introduction of the new Lucas L679 stop/tail light and alloy mounting

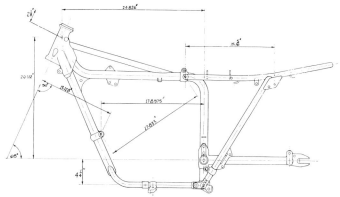

The additional frame stiffening strut previously specified for sports and competition model was now integrated into the actual frame design (From Eng No. H40528)

12 volt battery and Zener diode introduced on 1966 models. The earthing wire mounted between the diode and heat sink caused epidemic diode failures until earthed beneath the diode fixing nut

▼

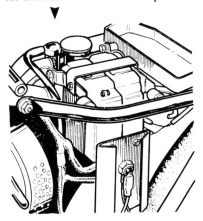

Yale-type ignition key introduced in 1966

Fuel Tank

Two entirely new fuel tanks were introduced for 1966, a 3 (imp) gallon for UK and General Export T100 models and a $2^1/2$ US gallon small sports tank for both US road and competition models, which no longer sported a tank top parcel grid. Both tanks were fitted with chrome quick-release filler caps, the US competition versions additionally incorporating a cap-retaining jack chain. New style 'winged' emblem tank badges were introduced, together with a new type of 'stick-on' knee grip, on the larger T100 fuel tank. The previous type of screw-on knee grip were retained on the smaller US competition tank. Only the T100 tank now specified a tank top seam chrome styling strip, all other trim having now been discontinued. A single corked tap provided main and reserve supply on the T100 tank, the US smaller size tanks being fitted with separate main and reserve lever taps.

Oil Tank

A new 6 (imp) pint (3 US quart) rubber-suspended oil tank was now fitted, incorporating a separate drain plug and chrome quick release filler cap with conventional froth tower, but with a rear chain lubrication facility, adjustable from within the tank filler neck. With two upper rubber mounting points, the lower tank fixing comprised a hollow tubular extension locating over a resilient grommet mounted on a frame peg.

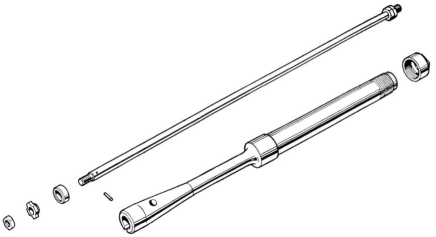

Exploded view of the telescopic fork hydraulic damper unit components as fitted to the US competition models

Brakes
As 1965 models.

Wheels
The Triumph design front and rear wheels continued for 1966 unchanged, apart from the introduction of a 'bolt-on' steel 46 teeth rear brake drum sprocket, eliminating the premature wear problem so often experienced with the previous integral cast iron version.

Tyres

UK and general export		Front	Dunlop 3.25 x 18 K70 Ribbed
		Rear	Dunlop 3.50 x 18 K70 Gold Seal Universal
USA	T100R & T100C	Front	Dunlop 3.25 x 19 K70 Ribbed
		Rear	Dunlop 4.00 x 18 K70 Gold Seal Universal
	T100C (East Coast)	Front	Dunlop 3.50 x 19 Trials Universal or Sports knobbly
		Rear	Dunlop 4.00 x 18 Trials Universal or Sports knobbly

Mudguards
As 1964 models.

Exhaust system
As 1964 models.

Air Filter
As 1965 models.

Electrical Equipment
This year saw the long overdue arrival of the 12 volt electrical system on the coil ignition equipped models, utilising the previous 120° dwell 4CA contact breaker and auto advance mechanism originally introduced in 1963. Early models utilised two Lucas MKZ9E 6 volt batteries in series (with a special carrier) until the Lucas PUZ5A 12 volt battery was introduced. Problems experienced with "random spark" pre-ignition caused early introduction of the replacement 160° dwell auto-advance cam unit number 54419254. No other change was made to the rotor, stator or rectifier, the 12 volt system output now being controlled by a newly introduced 12 volt zener diode. The SS700P headlamp continued, now with a pre-focus 50/40 watt head-lamp bulb and 6 watt pilot bulb.

Lighting and ignition switches continued to be fitted in the left side panel, with the main beam indicator and ignition warning lamps mounted in the headlamp shell. 12 volt ignition coils and horn were specified. Energy transfer ignition equipped models having no battery carrier, zener diode or rectifier continued unchanged, the stator feeding directly the 6 volt 24/24 watt headlamp bulb in the smaller headlamp unit which also mounted the Lucas PS6 lighting (LH) and dip (RH) switches. The handlebar carried the horn push and dip switch (LH) on T100 coil ignition models and the ignition cut-out button (LH) on the T100R and C models, with the horn button on the right-hand bar on T100C versions. All US models now specified an aluminium tail light adaptor bolted directly to the rear sports mudguard which supported the new Lucas L679 stop/tail light, tail lamp plate and rear number plate mounting bracket.

Speedometer and Tachometer

The Smiths magnetic speedometer and its rear-mounted speedometer drive gearbox introduced in 1964 was fitted to all road models. Competition models designed for the USA were equipped with VDO enduro-type instruments by the distributors, but did not have a tachometer. T100R road models this year were fitted with a new 10,000 rpm matching tachometer driven by a right angle screw-in drive gearbox (2:1) from the exhaust camshaft (RH) end. A tachometer was available as an 'extra' on T100 and T100C models.

Handlebars

$7/8$ inch sports bars continued unchanged from 1965. Ball ended clutch and front brake levers were still fitted only to US models with 'high-rise' handlebars. Moulded white rubber handlebar grips were now introduced.

Twinseat

As 1965 models

Finish	T100	T100R	T100C
Frame	Black	Black	Black
Forks	Black	Black	Black
Mudguards – front	Alaskan white, sherbourne green stripe, lined gold	Alaskan white, sherbourne green stripe, lined gold	Alaskan white, sherbourne green stripe, lined gold (except alloy)
– rear	Alaskan white, Sherbourne green stripe, lined gold	Alaskan white, Sherbourne green stripe, lined gold	Alaskan white, Sherbourne green stripe, lined gold (except alloy)
*Fuel tank	Sherbourne green and Alaskan white, lined gold	Sherbourne green and Alaskan white, lined gold	Sherbourne green with central Alaskan white racing stripe on tank top, lined gold
Oil tank	Black	Black	Black
Switch panel	Black	Black	–

*Top half colour of tank shown first.

Extras

Quickly detachable rear wheel
  (46T integral drum and sprocket)
Pillion footrests
Propstand
Twinseat safety strap
Tachometer.

US alternatives

US high rise handlebars
US brake throttle and clutch cables for above
Ball-ended clutch and front brake levers
Twinseat safety strap
Crankcase sump plate (T100C)
Folding footrests (T100C)

Left side view of the 1967 T100S Tiger 100 model now with Quiltop Twinseat

1967 model: Unit-construction T100S Tiger 100 model
Commencing Engine Number: H49833
Models: T100S
                T100T with T100R (Road) 'Daytona Supersports' and T100C
(Competition) 'Sports Tiger' variants for the US market.
Associated 'C' range models: T90 'Tiger 90'

Engine
The engine was uprated this year to specify twin $1^{1}/_{8}$ inch diameter choke Amal Monobloc carburettors on the UK and General Export T100T models, and on the US road model T100R Daytona super sports. Racing form (E3134) inlet camshafts were specified for all T100 models, whereas the single carburettor variants continued with (E3325) sports cam form exhaust camshafts

1967 also saw the introduction of the twin carburettor T100T model, the Tiger 100 Daytona shown here in UK trim. The Yale-type ignition switch was retained in the left side panel, and the lighting switch transferred to the headlamp

Right side view of the T100R Daytona Super Sports, now specifying 12 volt Siba ignition coils

with three quarter inch radius cam followers (tappets). The twin carburettor models specified (E3134) racing cam form exhaust camshafts, both inlet and exhaust, running in conjunction with four $1^{1}/8$ in radius cam followers. The exhaust camshaft now embodied an internally-machined tachometer drive slot. Another change related to the $1^{7}/16$ in. diameter inlet valves used on the single carburettor models which were increased to $1^{17}/32$ inch diameter for the twin carburettor models, the exhaust valves of all the variants remaining at $1^{5}/16$ in diameter, but made of a new, more heat resistant material. The aluminium alloy twin carburettor cylinder head was modified to accommodate a larger combustion sphere, thereby allowing the larger inlet valves and valve seats.

This change also permitted the single carburettor manifold to be standardised on the Tiger 90 variant, and the twin carburettor models to have separate left and right manifolds, with an inter-connected balance pipe. To improve the engine scavenge system, the oil pump scavenge plunger diameter was now increased from a nominal 0.437 in to 0.487 in. The new combustion spheres allowed the twin carburettor T100T and T100R models to be fitted with new 9.75:1 compression ratio Hepolite pistons.

In contrast the US competition variant, the Tiger 100C – the 'Sports Tiger' with Twinseat and upswept exhaust system.

Showing the twin Amal Concentric carburettor layout introduced on the 1968 range of models

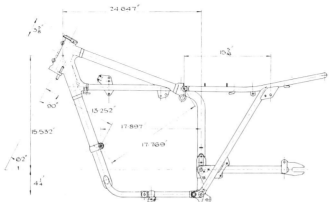

The revised frame assembly introduced from 1967, with modified headlug design and steering angle, and with rear frame stiffening bracket support for the swinging arm spindle

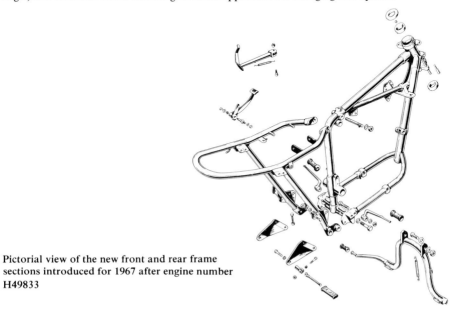

Pictorial view of the new front and rear frame sections introduced for 1967 after engine number H49833

Gearbox
As 1966 models but now with UNF mainshaft threads.

Primary Transmission
As 1966 models.

Frame
This year saw a complete revision of the front and rear frame, and the swinging arm assembly. A new front section with a fully-triangulated head lug having an integral top rail and bracing tank rail brought about a revised fork stem angle, from 65° to 62° to the horizontal. The associated rear frame section now carried 'out-board' triangular swinging arm pivot bracing plates, the stiffened swinging arm having been redesigned to accommodate a wide section tyre. The rubber-mounted 12 volt battery carrier and the 6 (imp) pint oil tank introduced in 1966 were fitted to the new frame, which carried a left-hand Lucas 41SA ignition switch (with Yale type lock barrel) fitted in a switch panel on coil ignition models, and a plain left-hand panel on energy transfer-equipped T100C models. Conventional painted steel front and rear mudguards were fitted to the T100S, T and R road models, polished stainless steel being used in the case of the T100C. A tool tray was bolted to the rear mudguard beneath the hinged Twinseat, the knurled chrome detachable anti-thief seat plunger knob having been replaced by a one-piece plastic-headed seat catch plunger. A new 'Easy-Lift' centre stand and a new propstand to suit the new frame assembly were introduced on all models, together with crankcase undershield (skid plate) and folding footrests on the T100C models.

Close-up of the rear frame swinging arm spindle support bracket

The new 1967 frame, fitted with US type competition forks and 'clamp-on' high-rise bars

Forks

New forks were introduced for 1967 having a new crown and stem to incorporate new rubber bush-mounted handlebars. The top fork lugs with their Yale type anti-theft steering lock were redesigned to suit the revised frame angle, although the fork covers, sliding members stanchions and fork internal continued from the previous year. The large chromed headlamp continued for the coil ignition models whereas the T100C competition models now fitted a new all-chrome detachable sports headlamp.

Fuel Tank

A revised three-point fixing design of 3 (imp) gallon petrol tank and smaller 2 $^1\!/_2$ (US) gallon tank were specified to suit the new front frame, with a chrome tank top parcel grid for the T100S and T models, no parcel grid being fitted on the US T100R and C tanks. Specification otherwise as the 1966 models.

Oil Tank

The previous year's 6 (imp) pint (3 US quart) rubber-suspended oil tank was fitted to the new frame.

Brakes

As 1965 models.

Wheels

Front as 1965, rear as 1966 models.

Tyres

UK and General	T100SS & T	Front	Dunlop 3.25 x 18 K70 Ribbed
Export		Rear	Dunlop 3.50 x 18 KG70 Gold Seal Universal
USA	T100R	Front	Dunlop 3.25 x 19 K70 Ribbed
		Rear	Dunlop 4.00 x 18 K70 Gold Seal Universal
	T100C	Front	Dunlop 3.50 x 19 Trials Universal or Sports knobbly
		Rear	Dunlop 4.00 x 18 Trials Universal or Sports knobbly

Mudguards

As 1966 models but the alloy mudguards were now replaced by stainless steel versions on T100C competition models.

Exhaust System

The previous twin downswept exhaust pipe and silencer system for the T100S and T100T models and straight-through silencer on the US T100R continued unchanged, whilst the 1967 T100C competition model was fitted with new dual upswept left-hand exhaust pipes and twin sports silencers.

Air Filters

Chrome pancake-type air filters were specified for all T100 models, the T100S having a felt element, the T100C a paper element and both twin carburettor T100T and T100R models coarse felt elements.

Electrical Equipment

The Lucas 88SA lighting switch was now housed within the headlamp, which also contained the ignition and hi-beam indicator lights. This was the last year of the energy transfer ignition T100 competition models. The handlebars carried the horn push and dipswitch (LH) and the new ignition cut-out button (RH) on coil ignition models, with the cut-out button on the right-hand handlebar and the lighting and dip switches in the headlamp shell in the case of the T100C model. UK and General Export models sported a rear number plate-mounted Lucas L564 stop tail lamp whereas the US models were fitted with the L679 type mounted on a polished alloy adaptor.

Speedometer and Tachometer

As 1966 models.

The 1967 US T100R Daytona specification with rigid handlebars, twin rotor twistgrip, ball end levers and matching speedometer and tachometer

Handlebars

The $^7/8$ in diameter touring handlebars previously used on the 3TA and 5TA models, now with rubber bush eyebolt mountings, replaced the previous sports direct fitting bars on the T100S and T100T models. They were fitted with an Amal adjustable friction twistgrip. The American 'high-rise' road and competition bars continued to be fitted to the T100R and T100C models. This year the white handlebar grips were dropped in favour of new shape 'cushioned' grips.

Twinseat

As 1965 models but now with a 'Quiltop' seat cover, with grey top, white piping, black sides and grey rim trim band, except US competition models, which has a black top and black rim trim band.

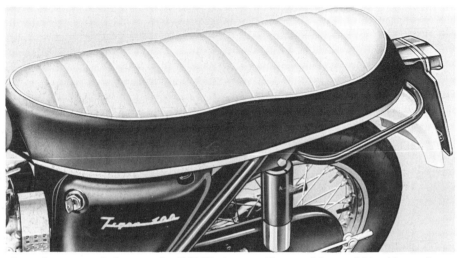

Illustrating the new Quiltop seat for 1967 (black top – US competition models), with grey lower trim band – black, US comp models

Finish	T100S	T100T	T100R	T100C
Frame	Black	Black	Black	Black
Forks	Black	Black	Black	Black
Mudguards – front	Alaskan white with pacific blue central stripe, lined gold	Alaskan white with pacific blue central stripe, lined gold	Alaskan white with pacific blue central stripe, lined gold	Polished stainless steel
– rear	Alaskan white with pacific blue central stripe, lined gold	Alaskan white with pacific blue central stripe, lined gold	Alaskan white with pacific blue central stripe, lined gold	Polished stainless steel
*Fuel tank	Pacific blue/ Alaskan white, lined gold	Pacific blue/ Alaskan white, lined gold	Pacific blue/ Alaskan white, lined gold	Pacific blue/ Alaskan white, lined gold
Oil tank	Black	Black	Black	Black
Switch panel	Black	Black	Black	Black

Top half colour of fuel tank shown first.

Extras

Quickly detachable rear wheel
  (46T integral drum and sprocket).
Pillion footrests.
Propstand.
Twinseat safety strap
Tachometer

US alternatives

US high rise handlebars.
US brake, throttle and clutch cables.
Twin rotor twistgrip
Ball-ended clutch and front brake levers.
Twinseat safety strap.
Chaincase sump plate (T100C)
Folding footrests (T100C)

Right side view of the 1968 T100S Tiger 100 model, now equipped with Amal Concentric carburettor, Lucas 6CA contact breakers with external condenser pack mounted beneath the fuel tank, the new 'shuttle-valve' front forks, and now housing the ignition switch in the left fork cover – with toggle type lighting switch in the headlamp

1968 model: Unit-construction T100S Tiger 100 model
Commencing Engine Number: H57083
Models: T100S
       T100T, with T100R (Road) 'Daytona Super Sports' and T100C
(Competition) 'Sports Tiger' variants for the US market.
Associated 'C' range models: T90 'Tiger 90'

Left side view of the 1968 T100T Tiger 100 Daytona, fitted with twin Amal Concentric carburettors. Note the introduction of the primary cover with rotor strobo-timing access. The Daytona model now featured an eight inch diameter full width hub front brake

Engine

The engine continued the previous year's specification, with twin new-type $1^{1}/_{8}$ in choke Amal Concentric carburettors having a connecting manifold balance pipe on the UK and general export T100T and US road model T100R Daytona Super Sports. The single carburettor models were fitted with a new 1 in diameter choke Amal Concentric instrument. The chrome plated pushrod cover tubes now dispensed with the bottom cup, the recently-introduced aluminium alloy cylinder head incorporating the $1^{7}/_{16}$ in diameter inlet valves on the single carburettor models and the $1^{17}/_{32}$ in

The US T100C featured legshields for the left side twin upswept exhaust system on the 'Sports Tiger'

The 1968 T100R for the US market, sold as the Daytona Super Sports, seen here in left side view

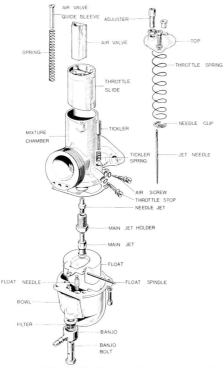

Exploded view of the Amal Type 900 Concentric carburettor introduced in 1968

diameter inlet valves on the twin were now standardised, the exhaust valves remaining at $1^5/16$ in diameter for all models. The rocker boxes, although visually unchanged from the previous year's models, were cast in much thicker section. No change was made to the cast iron cylinder barrel other than introduction of twelve point cylinder base fixing nuts. The crankcase assembly now incorporated a raised aluminium pad on the left-hand crankcase half below the cylinder base, to accommodate the rolled Triumph 'thief proof' engine numbering layout. The one-piece forged steel crankshaft with bolt-on flywheel, incorporating the revised '38° BTC location' slot, now carried second version heavier

131

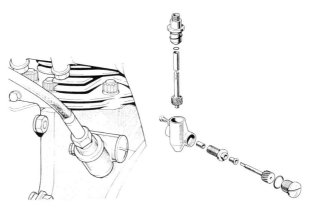

Illustrating the exhaust camshaft driven tachometer drive gearbox, and the '12-point' cylinder base nuts (note: the tacho gearbox introduced in 1966 had a RH thread into the crankcase until 1969, when it changed to a LH thread to prevent loosening)

duty connecting rods on twin carburettor models, also manufactured from RR56 aluminium alloy and fitted with Vandervell VP3 big end liners.

Gearbox

The Triumph four-speed gearbox continued unchanged, apart from the high gear which now incorporated a bronze bush that extended into the increased bore chaincase cover plate oil seal, to exclude road grit and the resulting excessive wear problems.

Primary Transmission

No basic changes were made within the primary transmission area for 1968, except that the 26 tooth engine drive sprocket no longer had a rotor drive peg facility, whilst the primary chaincase cover now included a rotor inspection cover revealing a fixed pointer to allow accurate stroboscopic ignition timing. A new rear sprocket cover plate behind the clutch contained a larger diameter oil seal to accommodate the new high gear extended bronze bush.

Frame

The new front frame introduced for 1967 continued into 1968, but the rear frame was again modified to incorporate two additional pegs on the left side backstay. They were used to spigot mount on rubber a new type left panel and toolbox, obviating the necessity for the previous mudguard-mounted tool tray. In addition, the battery carrier was changed from having a battery clamping arrangement to that of an integral plastic battery tray with a simpler rubber retaining strap.

Forks

1968 saw the introduction of the shuttle valve damper, UNF threads, sintered iron fork bushes (which were quickly dropped in favour of the original sintered bronze at H57470), extruded bottom outer members, and the steering damper discontinued henceforth on road models. The fork top covers now had headlamp alignment adjustment slots, the left-hand cover providing the mounting for the ignition switch. The large chromed headlamp continued for all road models, the T100C competition model having the smaller chrome, detachable, sports headlamp. Competition forks, and the front forks for the US road sports models, continued to be fitted with the steering damper and rigid clamp-mounted handlebars, whereas the UK and General Export models specified the Metalastic rubber bush-mounted handlebars.

Fuel Tank

The previous year's fuel tanks continued on the road and competition models for all markets, the only variation being the introduction at H60232 of much thicker 'stick-on' knee grips, and at H63307 bonded rubber '0' ring Stat-O-Seal sealing washers for the fuel taps. Also at H63307 the front tank mounting bolts were replaced by studs and 'Cleveloc' self-locking nuts.

The 1968 rear frame section incorporating peg spigot and rubber bush location of the toolbox side cover, with screwed knob attachment to the top rear frame rail

Oil Tank

A new 6 (imp) pint three point rubber-mounted oil tank was fitted, which reintroduced the lower return pipe 'twig' feed to the rocker oil feed pipe. It was fitted with a chrome quick release filler cap and the previous design of anti-froth tower, and had the rear chain oiler facility.

Brakes

The T100R and T100T models were now fitted with a front wheel incorporating an 8 in diameter single leading shoe brake, whilst the T100S and T100C models continued with the previously-specified full width 7 in brakes. No change was made to the rear brake options on any of the models in the range.

Wheels

As 1966 models except for the introduction of 8 in diameter full-width hubs on the T100T and T100R models.

Tyres

As 1967 models.

Mudguards

As 1966 models, the rear mudguard no longer having the previous tool tray mounting holes.

Exhaust System

The previous twin downswept exhaust system was modified to provide chrome cross bracing to the front engine mounting plate studs in lieu of the earlier lower frame braces. The internally-baffled silencers (mutes no longer available as an 'extra') continued for UK and General Export road models, the straight-through version silencers also continuing unchanged on the US road T100R model. The 1968 US T100C competition model continued with dual upswept left-hand exhaust pipes and twin sports silencers.

133

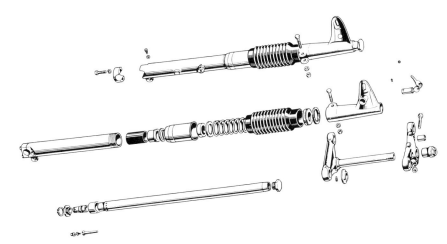

Exploded view of the 'shuttle-valve' front fork assembly introduced in 1968

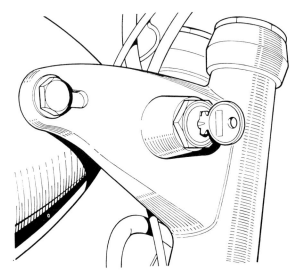

Location of the Yale-type ignition switch and 'slotted' front covers allowing increased headlamp adjustment

Air Filters
The only change related to the air filters fitted to the twin carburettor T100T and T100R models, which now had cloth and gauze elements.

Electrical Equipment
All models were now specified with a Lucas 12 volt coil ignition electrical system, fitted with a new Lucas 6CA contact breaker assembly and auto advance mechanism. A new contact breaker backplate permitted separate positional adjustment for each set of contact breaker points, which prevented the inclusion of integral condensers. In consequence a separate 2CP capacitor pack was introduced and fitted beneath the forward fuel tank mountings. The Lucas S45 ignition switch with 'Yale'-type key was now fitted to the left-hand front fork top cover and a Lucas toggle type 57SA lighting switch was mounted on the headlamp shell. Competition models continued to use the smaller diameter chromed headlamp incorporating ignition/oil pressure warning lamp and main beam indicator lamp, and the Lucas 57SA lighting (RH) and dip (LH) switches.

Speedometer and Tachometer
As 1966 models.

Handlebars
As 1967 models.

Twinseat
As 1967 models but now with a bright chrome rim trim band.

Finish	T100S	T100T	T100R	T100C
Frame	Black	Black	Black	Black
Forks	Black	Black	Black	Black
Mudguards – front	Silver with aquamarine central stripe, lined gold	Silver with aquamarine central stripe, lined gold	Silver with aquamarine central stripe, lined gold	Polished stainless steel
– rear	Silver with aquamarine central stripe, lined gold	Silver with aquamarine central stripe, lined gold	Silver with aquamarine central stripe, lined gold	Polished stainless steel
*Fuel tank	Aquamarine and silver, lined gold	Aquamarine and silver, lined gold	Aquamarine and silver, lined gold	Aquamarine
Oil tank	Black	Black	Black	Black
Side panel	Black	Black	Black	Black

*Top half colour of fuel tank shown first.

Extras
Quickly detachable rear wheel
(46T integral drum and sprocket).
Pillion footrests
Prop-stand
Twinseat safety strap
Tachometer

US Alternatives
US high rise handlebars.
US brake, throttle and clutch cables to suit above
Twin rotor twistgrip
Ball-ended clutch and front brake levers.
Twinseat safety strap.
Crankcase sump plate (T100C)
Folding footrests (T100C)
Friction steering damper (T100C)

1969 model: Unit construction T100 Tiger 100 model
Commencing Engine Number: H65573 to H67731 and subsequently date coded
series commencing XC06279 (10.12.68)

Models: T100S
T100T with T100R (Road) Daytona Super Sports and T100C
(Competition) 'Sports Tiger' for the US market.
Associated 'C' range models:- T90 Tiger 90

Right side view of the 1969 T100S single carburettor Tiger 100, now with the oil pressure indicator switch on the timing cover with new 'picture-framed' tank badges, and the tank top parcel grid having been discontinued. Also evident are the chromed spring rear suspension units and ball-ended handlebar levers, with the new twin leading shoe front brake shown to good effect. Not so evident in this photograph is the new coupled exhaust system

Left side view of the 1969 twin carburettor T100T Tiger 100 Daytona model. The illustration shows the new front hub with the chromed cover plate now featuring concentric ribs in lieu of the earlier flutes, but does not illustrate well the new coupled twin downswept exhaust system

Left side view of the 1969 US T100C Sports Tiger, still with twin left side upswept exhaust system, but now fitted with coupling junction in front of the silencer and with the chip-basket leg protector. The new prop-stand can be seen clearly in this photo

Left side view of the 1969 US T100R Daytona Super Sports. The US models now featured a chromed passenger grab rail bolted to the underside of the Twinseat.

Engine

The engine now incorporated a series of significant basic engineering changes, although continuing the previous year's specification. Nitrided heat-treated racing form (E3134) inlet camshafts were introduced on both single and twin carburettor models, with nitrided racing form (E3134) exhaust camshafts on twin carburettor models and nitrided (E3325) sports form exhaust camshafts on single carburettor T100S and T100C models. Cam followers were $1^1/8$ inch radius on the twin carburettor models and $3/4$ inch on single carburettor models. The new timing cover now incorporated an oil pressure indicator switch.

Twin and single carburettor road models continued to specify Hidural 5 bronze valve guides, but the US T100C single carburettor model now used cast iron inlet and exhaust valve guides. A new cast iron cylinder barrel of increased wall thickness was introduced, the crankcase assembly changing to accommodate the new one-piece forged crankshaft supported on a left-hand side roller and a right-hand side ball journal bearing. A change in the lubrication system fed the oil pump output to the

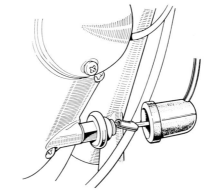

Close-up of the oil pressure switch introduced in 1969

Modifications to the tappet guide blocks to permit 'O' ring sealing, and push rod cover tubes with top locating 'fingers'

crankshaft assembly directly from the timing cover labyrinth, into the new crankshaft's extended shaft via a timing cover oil seal. At the same time, the opportunity was taken to introduce a revised oil pressure relief valve, now with UNF threads. The new left-hand crankcase was at last machined to accept the new left-hand threaded tachometer drive gearbox adaptor to finally overcome loosening in service. The new crankshaft retained the earlier 'bolt-on' cast iron flywheel incorporating the 38°BTC finder slot, which was now a new forging. A third version of heavy duty connecting rod was specified for the twin carburettor models, manufactured in RR 56 aluminium alloy and fitted with Vandervell VP3 big end liners. The T100S and T100C models were now converted to UNF thread sizes.

Gearbox
The gearbox continued unchanged and apart from using a new combination of location plunger and spring to give lighter loading of the gearbox camplate but more positive location.

Primary Transmission
The combined clutch housing and chain wheel no longer had cast-in pockets but was individually balanced. The chaincase cover now incorporated a detachable rotor cover (with Triumph motif) and at H65011 an ignition pointer was added, to be used in conjunction with a scribed line now introduced on to the rotor, for stroboscopic timing.

Frame
1969 saw the introduction of yet another new front frame section, comprising a modification of the extension of the head lug steering lock plunger platform to prevent accidental steering lock misuse and consequent steering problems. The rear frame swinging arm and centre stand continued unchanged into 1969 except that the UK and General Export models changed over to chrome un-shielded 145 lb per in rate springs, the US models adopting a 100 lb per in rate. The propstand changed to one with an increased strength section having a curved end, thereby dispensing with the 'flip-up' foot, and permitting more ground clearance, were the oil tank and battery box rubber-mounted in a manner identical to that of the previous year.

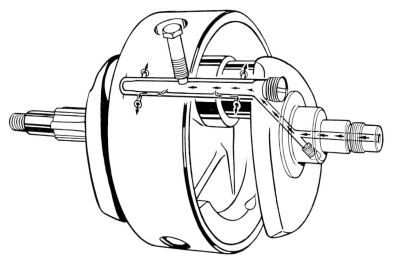

The 'ball and roller' crankshaft assembly introduced in 1969

Close-up of the new twin leading shoe front brake and air scoop anchor plate assembly   139

Forks

New front forks introduced for 1969 had increased fork stanchion centres (from $6^1/2$ in to $6^3/4$ in) to allow a wider section tyre to be fitted to the front wheel. This necessitated a new fork crown and stem together with associated top lug. The fork stanchion tubes, springs, damping components, outer members and top covers remained unchanged.

Fuel Tank

This year the famous Triumph tank top parcel grid was deleted from the specification of all models as a safety measure, following what was known in-house as the US 'caught' case. This change, requiring new road and competition tanks, saw the introduction also of a new tank badge, the Triumph motif itself now inset within a square picture frame border. Otherwise the fuel tank used on the road and competition models remained almost exactly as the previous year, except for the chrome top seam centre styling strip which was now hook-mounted to ease production and overcome cracking problems in service.

Oil Tank

No change was made to the previous year's oil tank for 1969.

Brakes

Front:	Full width heavily finned front hub, now with 8 in fully floating twin leading shoes on the T100T and T100R models, and 7 in fully floating twin leading shoes on the T100S and T100C competition models. The anchor plate incorporated the external twin cam linkage and a chromed wire mesh air scoop cover.
Rear:	As 1965 models.

Wheels

All front wheels were now fitted with a longer front wheel spindle to accommodate the 1969 increased centres front fork. Alternative internal grease retainers were fitted and a new chrome cover plate was featured incorporating concentric ribs in lieu of the previous plain chromed surface. The rear wheel continued unchanged.

Tyres

As 1966 models.

Mudguards

Chromed front mudguard stays were now specified on the T100R, the back stay no longer functioning as a front stand.

Exhaust System

A new twin downswept exhaust system, with a forward located coupling pipe, was introduced, the previous internally baffled US silencers being specified for the UK and General Export road models. The straight through silencer continued unchanged on the US Daytona Super Sports T100R model. The 1969 T100C sports competition model now featured a revised dual upswept left-hand exhaust system, with lower end connector and separate upper and lower silencers. A chrome wire leg protector christened 'the chip basket' was introduced for both leg protection and as a design feature.

Air Filters

The T100S continued with a felt element, whereas coarse felt elements were introduced on the other models in the range.

Electrical Equipment
This year a new fully-encapsulated Lucas RM21 stator was introduced, feeding twin Siba type 32,000 ignition coils, triggered by the Lucas 6CA contact breakers in the engine timing cover. A separate 2CP capacitor pack was fitted beneath the forward fuel tank mountings. UK and general export machines were, however, fitted with Lucas type MA12 ignition coils. No other changes were made.

Speedometer and Tachometer
As 1966 models.

Handlebars
Ball-ended clutch and brake levers at last became standard equipment on UK and General Export models, otherwise there was no other change in specification.

Twinseat
This year all T100 variants standardised on a single version of the Triumph Twinseat with black 'Quiltop' cover, black piping and skirt, and bright chrome plated rim trim band. US models incorporated in addition a rear passenger chrome hand rail fitted to the underside of the seat's rear rim.

Finish	T100S	T100T	T100R	T100C
Frame	Black	Black	Black	Black
Forks	Black	Black	Black	Black
Mudguards – front	Silver with Lincoln green centre stripe, lined white	Silver with Lincoln green centre stripe, lined white	Silver with Lincoln green centre stripe, lined white	Stainless Steel
– rear	Silver with Lincoln green centre stripe, lined white	Silver with Lincoln green centre stripe, lined white	Silver with Lincoln green centre stripe, lined white	Stainless Steel
*Fuel tank	Lincoln green/ silver lined White	Lincoln green/ silver lined White	Lincoln green/ silver lined White	Lincoln green
Oil tank	Black	Black	Black	Black
Side panels	Black	Black	Black	Black

*Top half colour of fuel tank shown first.

Extras
Quickly detachable rear wheel (46 teeth integral drum and sprocket).
Pillion footrests
Prop stand
Tachometer.

US Alternatives
US high rise handlebars
US brake, throttle and clutch cables for above
Twin rotor twistgrip
Crankcase sump plate (T100C)
Folding footrests (T100C)
Friction steering damper (T100C)

Left side view of the 1970 T100S Tiger 100, featuring the adjustable stop bolt in the propstand. This year the passenger grab rail became part of the rear lifting handle and was no longer bolted to the Twinseat pan

1970 model: Unit-construction T100 Tiger 100 model
Commencing Engine Number: KD 27866
Models: T100S Tiger 100

> T100T Daytona Super Sports with T100R (Road) Daytona 500 and T100C (Competition) Trophy 500 for the US market

Engine

The Triumph engine continued with further changes for 1970. The nitrided inlet camshaft used on all models, with (E3134) racing cam form, now dispensed with the distributor skew drive, breather disc drive slots and central bore with breather vent. The exhaust camshafts on the twin now incorporated a screwed-in tachometer drive plug. The crankcase assembly, was again changed the left-handed half to remove the camshaft breather facility, in favour of a primary chaincase breather and baffle plate, and at the same time dispensing with the drive sprocket oil seal (the engine now breathing into the primary chaincase). The right-hand crankcase half was machined to dispense with the right main ball bearing abutment ring.

Gearbox

The Triumph four speed gearbox this year specified improved surface finish, shaved gas carburised nickel chrome steel gear pinions on the heavy duty mainshaft. A high precision camplate pressing was introduced part way through the season.

Primary Transmission

Primary drive continued as previously but the chaincase now incorporated the new baffle plate and engine breather system. The initial fill oil level remained unchanged.

Frame

No change was made to either front or rear frame sections, or to the swinging arm, centre stand or propstand apart from having an adjustable stop bolt for the last mentioned for 1970. Although given a new part number as the result of a change in production methods, the oil tank remained fully interchangeable with the 1969 version. On the US models the rear chain oiler and adjustment facility was dispensed with. The rear suspension units with chrome springs now featured extended sleeve spring adjusters to protect them from road dirt and grit.

Right side view of the 1970 T100T Daytona Super Sports model

Left side view of the same model

Forks
Detail improvements were made to the front forks, the major changes being the use of a new extruded front fork bottom outer member and the provision of two additional oil bleed holes in the fork stanchions. The traditional Triumph adjustable friction steering damper was now dropped completely and replaced on all models by a chrome fork stem top sleeve nut.

Fuel Tank
Although identical 3 gallon (imp) fuel tanks were utilised on all home and general export T100S and T100T road models, the differing part numbers signified the difference in paint style/finish, as did the part numbers for the US T100R road and T100C competition variants. Fuel tap arrangements continued as for the 1963 models.

Oil Tank
This year another new oil tank was fitted, a deeper drawn pressing, creating greater capacity, but   143

Right side view of the 1970 USA T100R Daytona 500 model, now featuring the new integral rear chromed lifting handle and passenger grab rail

remaining at 6 (imp) pints recommended fill. This tank was fully interchangeable with the previous two tanks, and was standardised on the US, UK and General Export models. The rear chain lubricant facility was no longer included. The oil tank froth tower breather outlet connected to the new engine breather through the primary chaincase, in turn joining a silver 'D'-shaped breather pipe attached to the left side of the rear mudguard.

Brakes
As 1969 models.

Wheels
As 1969 models.

No changes were made other than the conversion of the rear wheel internal and external threads to UNF.

Left side view of the 1970 US T100C Trophy 500, the rear mudguard breather pipe being clearly visible. The Quiltop seat now featured black pierced 'Ambla' as standard

The chaincase breather adaptor introduced from 1970 models onwards

Tyres
As 1966 models.

Mudguards
A new standardised painted steel sports type front guard was specified for the T100T, T100R and T100S models, with a polished stainless steel equivalent for the US T100C competition model. Significant changes from previous models were dispensing with the front number plate mounting hole piercing, and changing the rear stay fixing bolts from one central bolt to two separate bolts. The painted steel rear mudguard on the T100R, T100S and T100T models had modified hole piercing to accomodate the new 'D' section breather pipe and to match the new rear stays, which now incorporated the integral rear passenger grab rail, introduced last year as an additional feature, attached to the underside of the Twinseat. Identical changes were made to the polished stainless steel rear mudguard on the T100C competition models. The chrome rear mudguard stay that also functioned as the rear lifting handle, now had an added rear loop to provide a passenger grab handle.

Exhaust System
As 1969 models.

Air Filters
As 1969 models, but now with commonised cloth and gauze filter element.

Electrical Equipment
As 1969 models.

Speedometer and Tachometer
As 1966 models.

Handlebars
As 1967 models.

Twinseat
A change for 1970 occurred in that the seat pan itself dispensed with the rear passenger grab rail facility which was now incorporated into the design of the rear mudguard stays. The 'Quiltop' seat cover now featured black pierced Ambla as standard.

145

Finish	T100S	T100T	T100R	T100C
Frame	Black	Black	Black	Black
Forks	Black	Black	Black	Black
Mudguards – front	Jaccaranda purple with silver central band lined gold	Jaccaranda purple with silver central band lined gold	Jaccaranda purple with silver central band lined gold	Stainless Steel
– rear	Jaccaranda purple	Jaccaranda purple	Jaccaranda purple	Stainless Steel
*Fuel tank	Jaccaranda purple	Jaccaranda purple and silver, lined gold	Jaccaranda purple and silver waist band, lined gold	Jaccaranda purple and silver central racing stripe, lined gold
Oil tank	Black	Black	Black	Black
Side panel	Black	Black	Black	Black

*Top half colour of fuel tank shown first.

Extras

Quickly detachable rear wheel
  (46 teeth integral drum and sprocket)
Pillion footrests
Propstand
Tachometer

US Alternatives

US high rise handlebars.
US brake, throttle and clutch cables for above.
Twin rotor twistgrip.
Crankcase sump plate (T100C)
Folding footrests (T100C)
Friction steering damper

Left side view of the 1971 US T100C Trophy 500 model

Right side view of the 1971 T100R Daytona model for the USA. This year new direction indicator lamps and front fork rubber mounted headlamp brackets were fitted

1971 model: Unit-construction T100R Tiger 100 model
Commencing Engine Number: KE 00001
Models: T100R 'Daytona'
    T100C 'Trophy 500' (with UK and General Export variants of both the single and twin carburettor models).

Engine

The previous year's engine continued with revised Amal twin $1^1/8$ inch choke Concentric carburettors, the gauze strainer having been dispensed with in favour of a cast-in weir and a float bowl drain plug. The steel capped aluminium alloy push rods now operated within the new chrome-plated cover tubes that had reverted to oil drain holes rather than 'fingers'. The unchanged overhead valve mechanism was housed in new rocker boxes fitted with 'O' ring-sealed side plugs, removable to assist in accurate rocker clearance setting. A new integral 'one-piece' oil pressure release valve was introduced almost immediately, to be replaced in favour of the previously composite 1970 version for the next season. The one-piece forged steel crankshaft with 'bolt-on' cast-iron flywheel now carried re-designed even heavier duty RR56 alloy 'H' section connecting rods, using Vandervell VP3 big end liners.

Gearbox

As 1970 models.

147

Right side view of the 1971 T100R Daytona model supplied to both UK, US and General Export markets

Right side view of the 1971 T100C model, supplied to UK, US and General Export markets

Primary transmission
The primary drive continued exactly as previously. Initial oil fill recommendations were now reduced to $^1/_4$ pint (imp) – 150cc.

Frame
As 1969 models.

Forks
The 1971 forks were fitted with new rubber-mounted headlamp brackets. Road models had a chromed fork stem sleeve nut whilst the competition variants had a sleeve nut that permitted fitment of a steering damper, when required. No other changes were made.

Fuel tank
As 1970 models. Differing part numbers indicated the alternative paint styles for road and competition versions.

Oil tank
A third visually unaltered but slightly increased volume version of the oil tank was introduced, the third change in the last three years. It was fully interchangeable with the previous year's tank. Service literature now quoted the capacity as $5^1/2$ pints (imp), or 6 pints (US) in an attempt to eliminate overfilling. It was fitted with a quick release chrome filler cap and oil level dipstick.

Brakes
As 1969 models.

Wheels
Front as 1969, rear as 1970 models. The quickly-detachable rear wheel option was now discontinued.

Tyres
As 1966 models.

Mudguards
Painted steel sports type front mudguards were fitted to the twin carburettor road models, and their polished stainless steel equivalents to competition machines, which also now featured chrome front mudguard stays. A new type of painted steel rear mudguard (polished stainless steel on the competition model) was now required to accommodate the 'Umberslade' type rear stop/tail lamp support bracketry, which supported the rear direction indicator lamp unit stanchions. This year the rear mudguard stay also carried circular orange side reflectors.

The extended tapering cone silencers fitted to the home market models later in the 1971 season

Exhaust System
A new exhaust system was introduced on the UK and General Export T100R models comprising a coupled twin downswept exhaust system with much larger T120 Bonneville extended cone silencers that gave a reduced sound level output. The US T100 also featured new twin downswept coupled exhaust pipes, but continued fitting the straight-through silencers.

Air Filters

The chrome pancake type air filter was discontinued on the UK and General Export models in favour of a redesigned induction noise suppression air cleaner. The assembly incorporated a pancake-type filter element within the integral plenum chamber and fed via a horseshoe-shaped sound level reducing 'tuned' induction pipe. The US East and West Coast models continued to fit the previous year's pancake type air filter.

Electrical Equipment

The electrical equipment for 1971 now included new handlebar switch controls and associated front and rear direction indicator lamps. For this year the perenially unreliable ammeter was discontinued and no longer fitted in the headlamp shell. The Lucas type S45 ignition switch was relocated on the left side front fork cover. Orange side reflectors were standardised on both Home, General Export and US models. The lighting was controlled by a 3 position (off, pilot and head) headlamp-mounted Lucas 57SA toggle-type switch. Competition T100C models continued with the smaller chrome sports headlamp, now minus ammeter, but carrying the ignition (oil pressure), direction indicator and headlamp main beam indicator lamps, together with the Lucas 57SA lighting (RH) and dip (LH) switches. A new type of aluminium-cased switch console was fitted to the left and right handlebars with provision for a horn push, dip switch and headlamp flasher on the left, 'kill-button' and direction indicator switch on the right. All models now specified the new rear tail lamp support bracket-mounted Lucas L679 stop and tail lamp, and side plate-mounted rear number plate.

Speedometer and Tachometer

No changes were made apart from the fitting of a Smiths speedometer and matching tachometer (when specified) with a new type of dial.

Handlebars

New handlebars were required to accommodate the new switch consoles, rubber-mounted on the road touring UK version and General Export T100R and T100C models. A solid mounting was employed on the 'western' version US road and competition models.

Twinseat

As 1970 models.

Finish	T100R	T100C
Frame	Black	Black
Forks	Black	Black
Mudguards – front	Olympic flame with black centre stripe, lined white	Polished stainless steel
– rear	Olympic flame with black centre stripe, lined white	Polished stainless steel
Fuel tank	Olympic flame with broad black waist band, lined white	Olympic flame
Oil tank	Black	Black
Side panel	Black	Black

Extras	US alternatives
Pillion footrests	US high rise handlebars
Propstand	US brake and throttle cables for above
Tachometer on competition models	Twin rotor twistgrip
	Alloy ball ended levers
	Crankcase sump plate (T100C)
	Folding footrests (T100C)
	Friction steering damper (T100C)

Right side view of the 1972 T100R Daytona model supplied to the UK and General Export market

1972 model: Unit construction T100R Tiger 100 model
Commencing Engine Number: JG 32303
Models: T100R Daytona

　　　　T100C Trophy 500 (with UK and General Export variants of both the single and twin carburettor models).

Engine
The overall specification of the T100R and T100C models remained unchanged for 1972 with the exception of the introduction of 'push in' exhaust pipes, and reverting to the earlier composite oil pressure relief valve.

Gearbox
The 1971 four-speed gearbox now continued unchanged until production of the T100 models ended in 1973.

Primary Transmission
No change was made to the primary transmission components for 1972.

Frame
As 1969 models.

Right side view of the 1972 US T100R Daytona model

Forks
As 1971 models.

Fuel Tank
As 1970 models.

Oil Tank
As 1971 model.

Brakes
As 1969 models.

Wheels
Front as 1969, rear as 1970 models.

Tyres
As 1966 models.

Mudguards
As 1970 models front, 1971 rear.

Exhaust System
The Triumph look was maintained by the addition of dummy finned exhaust pipe clips to the 'push-in'

exhaust pipes and the T120/T140 Bonneville heavier cone-shaped silencers introduced the previous year on UK and General Export Models were continued, with improved gas flow interiors. New and shorter coupled, downswept 'push-in' left and right-hand exhaust pipes, with straight-through silencers, were fitted to the US road T100R Daytona to (just!) meet new sound level legislation. Both the US and the Home and General Export T100C Trophy 500 models specified the new 'push-in' twin left-hand upswept pipes and coupled twin upper and lower silencers.

Air Filters
UK and General Export machines continued to specify the previous year's induction noise suppression air cleaners. The US models continued to fit the previous year's chrome pancake-type air filter.

Electrical Equipment
The electrical equipment was unchanged from the previous year's specification.

Speedometer and Tachometer
As 1971 models.

Handlebars
As 1971 models.

Twinseat
As 1970 models.

Finish	T100R	T100C
Frame	Black	Black
Forks	Black	Black
Mudguards – front	Cherry with cold white central band, lined gold	Polished stainless steel
– rear	Cherry	Polished stainless steel
*Fuel tank	Cherry and cold white lined gold	Cherry and cold white, lined gold
Oil tank	Black	Black
Side panel	Black	Black

*Top half colour shown first.

Extras
Pillion footrests
Propstand
Tachometer on competition models

US alternatives
US high rise handlebars
US brake and throttle cables to suit above
Twin rotor twistgrip
Alloy ball-ended levers
Crankcase sump plate (T100C)
Folding footrests (T100C)
Friction steering damper (T100C)

153

Right side view of the 1973 T100R Daytona model supplied to the UK. This year there were new fork top covers, new fork bottom sliding members, a new series of 3 and 2$^1/2$ gallon fuel tanks (without top seam), chromed front and rear mudguards, reversions to standard pancake-type air filters and a new type tachometer drive box. The UK models featured matt black painted front brake anchor plates with polished outer rim.

1973 model: Unit construction T100R Tiger 100 model
Commencing Engine Number: JH 15597
Models: T100R Daytona (with UK and General Export variants).
Associated Model: TR5T Trophy Trail

Engine
The T100 this year continued as the Tiger 100 model only in Daytona form, the new competition variant using an entirely new oil-in-frame layout. Twin 1$^1/8$ in diameter choke Amal carburettors with connecting manifold balance pipe were fitted to the T100R Daytona road model, and a single 1 in diameter choke carburettor on the TR5T model. The TR5T of necessity had alternative central cylinder head studs, modified rocker boxes and extended central cylinder head nuts to facilitate engine removal and replacement with the new increased diameter top tube oil-containing frame. No other changes were made.

Gearbox
The four-speed gearbox continued unchanged. The twin carburettor model continued to be fitted with road ratio gears, whilst the new TR5T model was specified with a close ratio gearset incorporating a special combination high gear layshaft/mainshaft pair.

Primary Transmission
As 1971 model.

Frame
No change whatsoever was made to the previous front and rear frame sections, the swinging arm, centre and propstand also remaining unchanged. An entirely new frame containing the engine oil compartment was introduced with the TR5T model, but is not the subject of this analysis.

Forks

Two changes were made to the T100R forks for 1973, new left and right-hand top covers, with reinforcement of the headlamp-mounting slots, and amended left and right-hand fork bottom sliding members. An entirely different fork with alloy top and bottom yokes, taper roller headraces, and no steering damper, but with alloy sliding outer members was used on the TR5T model.

Fuel Tank

New 3 (imp) gallon UK and General Export and $2^1/_2$ US gallon fuel tanks were introduced, dispensing with the top weld seam, and decorative chrome styling strip. UK and General Export models continued with a single main/reserve fuel tap and the US models with separate main and reserve lever taps. US models were finished in Hi-Fi vermilion and ice white, whilst UK and general export models were painted astral blue and gold, both variants carrying orange side reflectors on the front tank mountings.

The US variant of the 1973 T100R Daytona model

Oil Tank

As 1971 model.

Brakes

Front: As 1969 models, but with a matt black painted (UK and General Export) or polished (US) anchor plate rear as on 1970 models.

Wheels

Front as 1969 models, rear as 1970.

Tyres

All models	T100R	Front Dunlop 3.25 x 19 K70 Universal
		Rear Dunlop 4.00 x 18 K70 Universal
	TR5T	Front Dunlop 3.00 x 21 Trials Universal
		Rear Dunlop 4.00 x 18 Trials Universal

Mudguards

This year, chrome plated steel front and shortened rear sports type mudguards were introduced, the front with chrome front stays, the rear with a chrome plated combined rear stay and lifting handle now   155

Our favourite Tiger 100 engine-gearbox unit powering the new 1973 TR5T Trophy Trail model

modified to provide rear direction indicator lamp mountings that replaced the previous orange side reflectors. A long version rear mudguard was specified for some general export models. A new Lucas L917 rear stop/tail lamp incorporating side reflectors was supported on a new polished aluminium casting.

Exhaust System
As 1972 models.

Air Filters
As 1970 models, the UK noise suppression equipment now being discontinued.

Electrical Equipment
The only change related to the introduction of longer switch levers now with the 'kill button' on the left, dipswitch on the right and the use of a new Lucas L917 rear stop/tail lamp.

Speedometer and Tachometer
The Smiths tachometer was now fitted as standard equipment and it was driven by a new 2:1 exhaust camshaft driven right angle (LH adaptor) gearbox. Its 'one-piece' body housed the captive driven gear which was retained by a base welch washer, but nevertheless remained fully interchangeable with its predecessor.

Handlebars
All models now specified the new type of chromed steel ball ended control levers, the only change in 1973.

Twinseat
As 1970 models.

Finish	T100R (US)	T100R (UK and General Export)
Frame	Black	Black
Forks	Black	Black
Mudguards – front	Chromed steel	Chromed steel
– rear	Chromed steel	Chromed steel
*Fuel Tank	Ice-white/Hi-fi vermillion with black separating line	Gold/astral blue with black separating line
Oil tank	Black	Black
Side panel	Black	Black

*top half colour shown first.

Extras
Pillion footrests
Propstand.

US Alternatives
US high rise handlebars
US brake and throttle cables to suit above
Twin rotor twistgrip
Alloy ball-ended levers

Right side view of the 1974 T100R UK Daytona series 1 model – with black front brake anchor plate and 'torpedo'-type silencers, front and rear number plates

Right side view of the 1974 T100R US Daytona series 1 model, also displaying black front brake anchor plate and the 'torpedo'-type mufflers

1974 model: Unit construction T100R Tiger 100 model
Commencing Engine Number: JJ 57337
Models: T100R Daytona-Series 1 (with UK and General Export variants)
    T100D 'Daytona' Series 2 (disc front brake)
    (Pilot pre-production batch only completed).
Associated Model: TR5T Trophy Trail & Adventurer.

The 1974 T100R Series 1 models commenced manufacture in mid-1973, production ceasing abruptly with the NVT closure of Meriden on 14th September 1973. These models were virtually a continuation of the 1973 version. The ill-fated Series 2 variant, the T100D, with alloy front forks, disc front brake and a number of major engine improvements, sadly never saw the light of day apart from a partially-completed pre-production pilot batch of 18 machines (JJ57989 to JJ58006) awaiting completion on the day of closure.

Engine
The only modification for the 1974 season related to the oil pressure relief valve which now maintained 75/85 lb/sq in oil pressure and was fitted with a coarse mesh filter gauze.

Gearbox
As 1971 models.

Primary Transmission
As 1971 model.

Frame
As 1969 models.

Forks
As 1973 models.

158

Left side view of the proposed T100R Daytona series 2 model – intended for the UK and General Export markets. It featured an alloy front fork, front disc brake, alloy rear hub, and commonised 650/750cc model silencers.

Fuel Tank
As 1973 models, apart from colour scheme.

Oil Tank
As 1971 model.

Brakes
As 1973 models.

Wheels
Front as 1969 models, rear as 1970.

Tyres
All models	Front	Dunlop 3.25 x 19 K70 Universal
	Front	Dunlop 4.00 x 18 K70 Universal
TR5T	Front	Dunlop 3.00 x 21 Trials Universal
	Rear	Dunlop 4.00 x 18 Trials Universal

Mudguards
As 1973 models.

Exhaust System
'Push in' coupled exhaust pipes continued to be specified for 1974. However, to cope with the ever increasing stringency of reduced sound level requirements, new pencil-slim torpedo-shaped silencers were standardised for all markets. They were attached by slide-in captive-head fixing bolts to new style silencer brackets similar to those of the T120/T140 models for this year.

Air Filters
As 1970 models.

159

Electrical Equipment
As 1973 models.

Speedometer and Tachometer
As 1973 models.

Handlebars
As 1973 models.

Twinseat
As 1970 models.

Finish

	T100R
Frame	Black
Forks	Black
Mudguards – front	Chromed steel
– rear	Chromed steel
*Fuel tank	Ice white/argosy blue, lined in gold
Oil tank	Black
Side panel	Black

*Top half colour shown first

Extras
Pillion footrests.
Propstand.

US alternatives
US high rise handlebars
US brake and throttle cables to suit above
Twin rotor twistgrip

The intended US variant of the 1974 T100 Daytona series 2 model which, sadly, was never to see the light of day

Continuing for 1974, the TR5T Trophy Trail sister model (sold this year as the Adventurer)

Right side view of the 1974 TR5T Adventurer

Technical Data
Major Part Numbers
Year-by-Year

A fully comprehensive 24 page part numbered specification for each year of manufacture of the pre-unit and unit construction Tiger 100 and Daytona models, designed to be used in association with this Development History has been made available in matching booklet form, and is printed and published in conjunction with this book by J R Technical Publications Limited, Common Lane Industrial Estate, Common Lane, Kenilworth, Warwickshire, CV8 2EL, under their part number JRP026,

The booklet provides over two hundred and seventy lines of specification in recognised replacement parts list headings, with individual component part numbers for each years models between 1939 and 1974. In addition are two pages listing important part number identification and recommended combinations of close and wide ratio gears and their corresponding ratios together with helpful data detailing the identification of appropriate alternator rotors and stators (with associated wiring colour coding).

A few years of the Tiger 100/Daytona . . .

Right side view of the 1946 Tiger 100. The 'cocktail shaker' silencers were now replaced by a more conventional design

Right side view of the 1947 Tiger 100

Right side view of the 1951 Tiger 100

Right side view of the Tiger 100 fitted in racing trim

164   Right side view of the 1961 US T100A model

Buddy Elmore – first across the finishing line in the 1966 Daytona 200 mile experts race.

Right side view of the 1966 West Coast US T100C

Right side view of the 1967 T100S, showing clearly the new rear frame section. Note also the UK models continued to carry front and rear registration number plates and associated rear stop/tail lamp

The Best Motorcycle
in the World

Left side view of the 1969 US T100C Trophy 500 model

Right side view of the 1970 T100S single carburettor Tiger 100, with the new 'extruded' front fork bottom outer members

Later 1971 season's T100R models for the UK market introduced 'sound level' equipment comprising carburettor inlet 'snorkels' and long tapering cone silencers

167

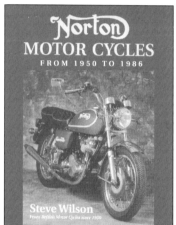
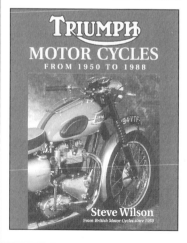